WINGS OF WAR

WINGS OF WAR

Fighting WWII in the Air

JEFFREY L. ETHELL

Naval Institute Press   *Annapolis, Maryland*

Library of Congress Cataloging-in-
Publication Data

Ethell, Jeffrey L.
    Wings of War: Fighting WWII in the
air / Jeffrey L. Ethell.
        p.   cm.
    ISBN 1-55750-249-8
    1. World War, 1939–1945—Aerial
operations, American—Pictorial works.
I. Title.
D790.E85   1994
940.54'4973—dc20   93-20957

Printed in the United States of America
on acid-free paper ∞

9 8 7 6 5 4 3 2

First printing

Don't give me an old Thunderbolt
It gave many a pilot a jolt.
It looks like a jug
And it flies like a tug,
Don't give me an old Thunderbolt.

Don't give me a P-38
With props that counter rotate.
She'll loop, roll and spin
But she'll soon auger in,
Don't give me a P-38.

Don't give me a P-51,
It was all right for fighting the hun.
But with coolant tank dry
You'll run out of sky,
Don't give me a P-51.

Just give me operations
Way out on some lonely atoll,
For I am too young to die,
I just want to go home.

"GIVE ME OPERATIONS," WORLD WAR II
ARMY AIR FORCES BALLAD

I am convinced that the growing air power of Japan will be the decisive element in the mastery of the Pacific. . . . Air operations for the destruction of Pearl Harbor will be undertaken. . . . Aeronautical siege will then be inaugurated against all the Hawaiian Islands and all vessels approaching will be attacked through the air or under the water. . . . The air attack to be made on Ford's Island at 7:30 A.M. Route to be direct. . . . The Philippines would be attacked in a similar manner.

Brig. Gen. William Mitchell, assistant chief, U.S. Army Air Service, Secret Report, 24 October 1924

CONTENTS

ACKNOWLEDGMENTS

Such a look into the heart of World War II would have been impossible without the vast panorama of people willing to contribute. My very able research and writing assistants, Jennie and David Ethell, bore the brunt of sorting, cataloging, and entering great gulps of material, much painstakingly transcribed from taped reminiscences and interviews. The available data bank soon became rich through their efforts . . . and working with my kids, accomplished and published writers themselves, enriched my own life. What a great summer of '92 we had together!

Those who fought the war, remembered it, and took the Kodachromes are very special people. Without exception they were generous beyond measure, thus increasing our historical consciousness of the war immeasurably. Hank Redmond, Stanley J. Wyglendowski, Francis M. Grove, R. T. Smith, Richard H. Perley, and Kenneth I. Kailey (with the late Robert R. Frizell's slides) not only provided their invaluable slides but also often sent reams of recollections, certainly above and beyond . . . well, I don't want to sound too close to all that wartime decoration terminology, but they sure made the book sing.

The rich Kodachromes taken by people during their tours gave the book its reason for being—my thanks to all of you: Byron Trent, Carroll S. Barnwell, Dorothy Helen Crowder for providing her late husband J. P.'s slides, Alexander C. Sloan, L. Jeffrey French, Vivian Lewis for providing her late husband T. K.'s slides, Robert Astrella, Link Derick, Ole C. Griffith, Paul A. Thomas and Bob Rickard, Arnold N. Delmonico, Edward W. Simpson, Jr., Fred E. Bamberger, Jr., Calvin Bannon, George Saylor, Charles Jaslow, Maurice DeLay, James M. Stitt, Jr., Joseph S. Kingsbury, James Wilson, Edward Kregloh, John L. Lowden, Victor W. Tatelman, John P. Bronson, John A. Worth, George J. Fleury, Edward F. Egan, Dennis Glen Cooper, Arthur O. Houston, Herbert R. Rutland, Jr., Edward B. Richie, and Richard Davidson for helping his father Morris send his slides.

Stories poured in from a great host of veterans, adding intense mental color to enhance the visual color. I mourn the loss of some who became close friends and never had the pleasure of seeing their work in print. All of you were superb—Gil C. Burns, Jr., Milt Miller, Ken Hamilton, Mark Shriver, Walter E. Ohlrich, Jr., Jack Hoey, James Hanson, Stan Hutchins, Robert E. Fitzhugh, the late Bernie Lay, Jr., David McCampbell, the late Carroll R. "Andy" Anderson, Don Lopez, Enver "Ed" Curry, Henry Straub, John Stege, Milton W. Sanders, Howard M. Park, F. Henri Henriod, Heinz Knoke, Saburo Sakai, Robert Nourie, Bud Abbot, James A. Gill, Ralph J. Watson, Jr., for sending his father's letters and diaries, Scott McCuskey, John A. Tilley, Dean Laird, and the late Frank C. Shearin, Jr.

With the selflessness of others in both getting slides duplicated and loaned, as well as sending recollections from other veterans, much of the book would have been impoverished. You really came through—Paul Lawrence; Stan Piet; John and Donna Campbell; Roger A. Freeman; George Hicks of the Airmen Memorial Museum; Bob DeGroat; Alfred Price; John Stanaway; Mark Hutchins; Fred Alexander; William H. Bartsch; Fred Roos; Frederick A. Johnsen; David Ostrowski; Tom Doll; Lockheed Aircraft Corporation; the great National Air & Space Museum research and photo crew of Dan Hagedorn, Mark Avino, Melissa Keiser, Tim Cronen, and Larry Wilson; Larry Davis; Bill Bielauskas; Steve Birdsall; William N. Hess; Duane J. Reed at the U.S. Air Force Academy; Charles O'Mahony; Donald A. Soderlund, Jr.; and Paul Stillwell and Linda W. O'Doughda of the U.S. Naval Institute Oral History Program.

Permission to quote recollections from other sources was, without exception, enthusiastic. You made the book all that much better.

Charles A. Watry for *Washout!* California Aerodrome Press, P.O. Box 1365, Carlsbad, California 92008.

Robin Higham for Donald Marks, Keith Matzinger and Carl Fritsche in *Flying Combat Aircraft of the USAAF-USAF*. Copyright 1978, reprinted with permission of Sunflower University Press, Manhattan, Kansas 66502.

Barrett Tillman for Tommy Blackburn in *Corsair: The F4U in World War II and Korea*. Naval Institute Press, Annapolis, Maryland, 1979.

Charlie Henderson in *Avenger at War*. Naval Institute Press, Annapolis, Maryland, 1991.

James F. Sunderman for James Bellah, Dennis McClendon, Kenton McFarland, Manford Susman in *World War II in the Air: Europe—The Pacific*. Franklin Watts, Inc., New York, New York, 1962, 1963.

W. W. Norton and Co. for Bert Stiles in *Serenade to the Big Bird*. Copyright 1947 by Mrs. Bert W. Stiles.

Peter Kilduff for Norman Sterrie, Max Leslie, Bud Furney in *U.S. Carriers at War*. Stackpole Books, Harrisburg, Pennsylvania, 1981.

E. Earle Rogers II for Marion Carl in *Foundation*. Naval Aviation Museum Foundation, P.O. Box 33104, NAS Pensacola, Florida 32508.

Naval Institute Press for Jack Coley, C. J. Graham in *PBY: The Catalina Flying Boat* by Roscoe Creed. Annapolis, Maryland, 1985.

Steve Millikin for Bob Dosé, Bob Butcher in *The Hook*. The Tailhook Assn, Box 45308, NAS Miramar, San Diego, California 92145.

PHOTO CAPTIONS:

PAGE I: A brand-spanking-new replacement P-51D Mustang, just delivered to the 355th Fighter Group at Steeple Morden, mid-1944. With the coming of the Mustang and its ability to fly all the way to the targets with the bombers, the fighter pilots of the Eighth Air Force were able to roam Germany at will, seeking out the Luftwaffe in the air and on the ground. This was the long-range escort fighter so desperately needed when German pilots were hacking bombers out of the sky at a great rate . . . it didn't arrive a moment too soon. Though AAF prewar doctrine insisted bombers could defend themselves against enemy fighters, the skies over Europe proved just the opposite, and those commanders who refused to budge were relieved or transferred. ALEXANDER C. SLOAN

PAGE III: As American industry geared up for wartime production, the services struggled to match the output with qualified technical personnel. Soon schools for all manner of disciplines were running at full tilt, introducing men who had worked on farm tractors—and those who had never seen one—to maintaining complex bombers and fighters. These men are working on a training airframe Flying Fortress at Randolph, learning the intricacies of what makes Wright engines and General Electric turbos work. LESLIE BLAND VIA MAURICE DELAY COLLECTION

PAGE IV: Although Italy could be a mud bog in the summer and a snow belt in the winter, it was a beautiful place to be at times. This sunset over the 37th Squadron, 14th Fighter Group base at Triolo catches a late-working crew chief with the cowlings off the right engine. It really didn't matter whether they wanted to go in and get some chow or not—if the airplane was to be on the line for the next day's mission, the ground crew had to get the airplane ready, often outside in the dark. Sunsets were something to behold, but they could be enjoyed for only a few minutes, sometimes with mixed feelings, because they usually meant time was running out. JAMES STITT

PAGE V: A newly delivered P-40E on the ramp at Martin State Airport, Baltimore, awaits a pilot from the 33rd Fighter Group in March 1942. The AAF medium green and sand, with blue undersurfaces, camouflage reflects the British influence in paint—lend-lease Kittyhawks were being built on the same Curtiss assembly line. But even lend-lease aircraft became fair game for an expanding U.S. war machine . . . once Americans were in it for keeps, most aircraft manufacturers filling foreign orders were told to sell their products to the home team. J. P. CROWDER VIA DOROTHY HELEN CROWDER

PAGES VI–VII: Bob Younger flies a 12th Bomb Group B-25J over the deltas near Fenny, India, with the window open in an undershirt . . . it was hot and humid, and stateside regulations were not considered of great importance when it came to staying cool. According to navigator Hank Redmond, "Our daily missions were to depart from Fenny, climb out and fly over the mountains between our base and Burma, drop down to bombing altitude, and then release our bombs. On return we had to climb back over the mountains to get back to our base . . . an engine out was always a great fear as climbing to enough altitude through thunderstorms that would build up in the early afternoon was more than risky." HANK REDMOND

PAGE VIII: A veteran 7th Photo Group F-5 at dispersal, Mt. Farm, late 1944. American synthetic haze paint was very close to PRU Blue, except that it was multishaded to compensate for sunlight and shadow. It worked just as well at altitude, but when worn sections were oversprayed, as seen on the nose, the new paint was always darker and didn't match. After a while no one really cared, and in the end combat aircraft of all types were left unpainted natural metal. Camouflage didn't really seem to make much difference in combat, and leaving it off resulted in a weight savings of several hundred pounds and increased range. Nevertheless, these blue photo birds were some of the most attractive AAF aircraft flying. ROBERT ASTRELLA

PAGE X: When the 1st Air Commando Group formed under Cols. Phil Cochran and Johnny Alison, few had any idea it would be as successful as it was. Equipped with P-51 fighters, B-25 bombers, C-47 transports with gliders, L-5 liaison light aircraft, and a little bit of everything else, including the first military helicopters, the unit could undertake a variety of missions at a moment's notice. British Brigadier Orde C. Wingate used the unorthodox unit in support of his 77th Indian Brigade Chindits to fight the Japanese behind their own lines . . . a small force of Chindits at crucial points to make the enemy back away. This 1st ACG P-51A cruises over the Burmese landscape during an escort mission for the unit's B-25s. R. T. SMITH

PAGE XV: The North American SNJ Texan was America's most significant advanced trainer, flown by instructors like actor LT Robert Taylor, who served as a naval aviator during the war. NATIONAL ARCHIVES

PAGE XVI: The deck of the USS *Monterey* is a busy place during the initial raids against the Marshall and Gilbert Island chains, November/December 1943. NATIONAL ARCHIVES

PAGE XIX: LT Robert L. Brown puts the squadron mascot in the cockpit of his Hellcat for a publicity shot. NATIONAL ARCHIVES

PAGE XXI: The workhorse of World War II was the Douglas C-47 Skytrain, or Dakota to the British. It carried just about everything, from tools to troops, and towed gliders as well. "Mary Co-ED II" flew with the 74th Squadron, 434th Troop Carrier Group, through some of the toughest campaigns in Europe, as her mission tally attests. The unit took part in the airborne assaults on Normandy, Holland, and Germany, as well as flying into the middle of Bastogne to resupply American soldiers cut off by the Germans in the "bulge." This was more than dangerous, because the Gooney Bird was simply a converted civil DC-3 airliner . . . it didn't even have self-sealing fuel tanks, which resulted in many going down under enemy fire at low level. ROBERT ASTRELLA

PAGE 1: Fire fighters move down the ramp in front of a Vought SBU-2 just before the outbreak of World War II. ARNOLD/NASM

INTRODUCTION

There will never be another period in military aviation, or in military history for that matter, that equals World War II for scope, numbers, and impact on the world. Governments across the globe prepared for, fought, won, and lost a war that accelerated aeronautical research from the biplane era of wood and fabric into the jet age. Aircraft companies used to measuring a good production run in terms of two digits were called upon to build thousands of warplanes. New designs proliferated, some quite successful and far reaching, others bizarre. It was a time of almost unlimited money for better machines, forcing aeronautical engineers to reach for ever-higher performance in ever-shorter time spans.

Within the United States, military aviation struggled desperately to get out from under the isolationism of the 1930s. Budgets were pitifully small, providing little equipment and even less pay for those required to operate it. Most military planners saw what was coming and tried to prepare, often behind the scenes and without official approval, but 7 December 1941 still caught America without enough aircraft to fight the Axis powers. Even those machines available were, on the whole, obsolete. Yet by 1943, U.S. industrial power was harnessed. The mighty air fleets of 1944 and 1945, launched from both land and sea, were the largest ever assembled. Never again will nations fight air battles the size of those in the Second World War. By the time the Japanese surrendered, almost 300,000 American aircraft had been built during the war—more than double the run in Britain, almost triple that of Germany, and near a whopping five times the number pushed out in Japan. In March 1944 alone American workers built 9,113 airplanes.

Although interservice rivalry was an American way of life, when it came down to the line, both the U.S. Army and Navy were given almost an unlimited supply of funds to get the job done. The limiting factor was industrial capacity, though that expanded and, in fact, overtook the rest of world faster than any enemy of the United States had dreamed of in their worst fears.

Almost 70,000 aircraft were built for the navy. In December 1941, the navy had 8 battleships, 4 aircraft carriers, 1 escort carrier, and 486,266 personnel. By September 1945, the numbers had swelled to 5,788 warships, 66,000 landing vessels, 16 *Essex*-class carriers, more than 100 other carriers launched, and 4 million personnel, of which 400,000 (10 percent) served the air arm. The prewar Army Air Corps, with 20,196 in uniform (11 percent of the army) on 30 June 1938, grew into the massive U.S. Army Air Forces (USAAF), which six years later was swarming across the world with 2,372,292 people (31 percent of the army).

The American training program to get aircrew into army, navy, marine, and Coast Guard aircraft matched industry with a frenzy. In 1939 the U.S. Navy and Marine Corps had 2,100 aircraft flown by 1,800 pilots supported by 625 ground officers and 21,000 enlisted men. By 1945 the navy had trained slightly fewer than 65,000 naval aviators, the AAF had put more than 190,000 pilots and 400,000 aircrew in their aircraft, and women and minorities were becoming an integral part of the military machine.

The pilots and the planes of this incredible era were among the most colorful and captivating of aviation's very short history. Yet the mists of time and most published World War II photographic histories have caused public memory of this most massive of conflicts to fade into a black-and-white haze. Although the navy brass issued orders against painting anything personal on aircraft, many ignored the regs and decorated their machines. On the other hand, Army Air Forces crews were allowed to paint their aircraft in almost any fashion they wished, giving rise to groups of bombers and fighters that made Baron von Richthofen's Flying Circus pale by comparison.

But who would really know that? Since the war, except in the memories of those who served in the military services during the early 1940s, those vivid images of combat have been etched in tones of gray, because both still photos and motion-picture film were shot in the primary medium of the day, silver nitrate–based black-and-white film. Even the most knowledgeable historians have taken for granted that succeeding generations will never see the war in color due to the assumed rarity of wartime color film.

I have to admit I was among those who thought wartime color film scarce, even after writing numerous books on World War II aviation history. By sheer hunch I began to ask veterans during interviews if they knew of any color film taken during the war. Within a very short time, the floodgates opened, and unimaginably pure Kodachrome slides and movies began to pour in. Much to my surprise, I was told this film was available on the drugstore shelf as early as 1935. Apparently, thousands of people went off to war with good cameras and Kodachrome. As of this writing, my collection of World War II color images has topped ten thousand, the largest such body of its kind in the world, and it grows weekly.

These sharp, striking photographs are a revelation, even after numerous viewings. Taken primarily as snapshots by people who were fighting a war, these Kodachromes have a rich human flavor that few professionals would have captured. No one was trying to create a scene or stage an action. This was World War II as it happened to men—mostly boys—and women away from home for the first time, goggle-eyed tourists, caught in events greater than themselves.

If you don't find a particular favorite aircraft or scene here, realize that the body of color work can't be compared to the wealth of black-and-white photography available. The humidity and heat of the Pacific were particularly brutal to Kodachrome, leaving, it appears so far, most of the surviving images to come out of Europe. Particularly frustrating is the relative scarcity of Kodachrome shot by U.S. Navy personnel attached to aviation units in comparison with those in the U.S. Army Air Forces. Even more maddening is the lack of U.S. Marine Corps color photography. As a result, any work of this type will naturally lean toward AAF activity.

Thankfully, people took Kodachrome to war, showing the historian and the reader that World War II was not fought in black and white. When matched with vivid first-person recollections of life in a world at war, these photos take on an intense reality, allowing a new generation to enter a world none thought possible to experience first hand . . . until now.

WINGS OF WAR

STATESIDE

Zone of Interior

GIL BURNS
P-47 pilot, 50th Fighter Group

Airplanes and flying were first introduced to me in 1933 at age eleven. It seems at that age many boys emerge from their childish cocoons and start eyeing more manly, more adventuresome pursuits. In 1933, without television and with only squeaky radios, the young boys' eyes were drawn to the newsstands in the local drug-stores. Row upon row of pulp magazines with their exciting covers in full color, with all sorts of heroes to choose from. Detective pulps with their gangster covers, western pulps with gun slinging Texas Rangers, and, best of all, the air war pulps.

World War I aircraft in mortal dogfighting combat, the most exciting of all the pulps! There were pulp titles such as *Sky Birds, Battle Birds, Flying Aces, Lone Eagle, Wings,* etc., etc. The pulp which probably thrilled the boys the most was *G-8 and His Battle Aces.* G-8 and his two sidekicks, Nippy Watson and Bull Martin, flew SPADs against the enemy from their airdrome at Le Bourget, Paris.

G-8 was the master spy and was usually dropped behind the German lines in disguise. His mission was to thwart an enemy scheme which was designed to defeat the Allies. Those were exciting stories, and I would go to sleep with visions of SPADs and Fokkers dancing in my dreams. The G-8 stories planted a seed in my brain, the romance of flight, one which was never to leave.

The reading of pulps was the inspiration for another hobby, model-airplane building. It was possible to make the very planes I was fantasizing about. The first attempts were planes of solid balsa wood, and next came flying models . . . rubber-band driven propellers and spars covered with tissue paper created great replicas. SPAD, Fokker, SE-5, Albatros, Pfalz, Camel, Nieuport—they were all hanging by threads from my bedroom ceiling in one huge, glorious dogfight.

BUD ABBOT
PT-22 pilot, primary training

We went through primary training at King City, a civilian contract school, in Ryan PT-22s. When we finished our required training flights, we still had time we had to fly to get our total hours for the class, so they just turned us loose solo. They'd say, "Okay, you take an airplane up there and fly for an hour, and get your time in."

The King City flying sector, as it was outlined, included a little valley called something like Bitterwater Valley, which was the furthest extreme of our flying area. The instructors never went over there because it was too far from the

A pair of BT-14 basic trainers skim the clouds above Randolph Field, Texas, just before the outbreak of war in the Pacific. This modern, low-wing monoplane brought the end of the bi-plane era to army fliers and propelled them into the real world of high-performance combat aviation. Flying airplanes like this, and its bigger brother the AT-6, was often more temptation than a yearning pilot could stand. The Depression era had denied youth its hot rods, so what bet-ter substitute than a powerful military airplane? Many were "washed out" for "flathatting" . . . flying too low, often under bridges and below the height of the buildings on main street.
LESLIE BLAND VIA MAURICE DELAY
COLLECTION

3

base, a waste of time just flying back and forth. When we were out solo, though, we said, "Let's go out to Bitterwater Valley, since the instructors never go over there. We can do a little dogfighting and have some fun!"

About five of us took off and flew over, playing "follow the leader." One of the guys spotted this big water tank. There were a bunch of cows laying on the ground around the tank, so he decided to go down and buzz the cows. He did, and then the next guy went down and buzzed the cows. Each guy's trying to get a little bit lower, when Cadet Anderson goes in.

Just as he flew over, one of the dairy cows stood up. One of the wheels of his undercarriage apparently hit the cow right in the middle of the back. This bounced him in the air about ten, fifteen feet and kind of shook him up a little bit, but he just kept on flying. He felt sure, though, that he'd wiped out the undercarriage as he headed back for the base.

He told us later, "I thought of all kinds of things. Well, maybe I'll just bail out and let the airplane crash; tell them that the engine had stopped or run out of gas. No, it didn't run out of gas, because they'd just refueled the airplanes. Couldn't use that excuse." The more he thought about it, the more he thought, "No, I'll just go back and face the music." He entered the traffic pattern, flew around, got a signal from the tower to land, and went on in, making the most beautiful landing he'd ever made, just feeling for the ground. The airplane landed okay. He taxied in, parked the airplane, jumped out, and took a look real quick. He couldn't see any damage, so he went on back into the ready room; didn't say a word.

The next morning, at breakfast, we were told that all of the senior class had to muster in the assembly hall right after breakfast. We all went in. The commandant, a Captain Kelly, got up on the stage and said, "Okay, we've got a problem. I've got to solve it right now. Will the cadet who killed the cow please stand up and acknowledge." We started looking at one another, and nobody said a word.

"Okay, now, this is your last chance. You know we're on the honor system. Now, will the cadet that killed the cow stand up and admit it?" Nobody moved. "If the cadet who killed the cow won't admit it, then, until he does, the entire senior class is restricted." We had two weeks left to go in the school, but nobody said a word. Then he started ranting. Oh, he was really mad. "We've checked all the airplanes, and we can't find out which airplane it was!"

Turned out the farmer had called. During the night, one of his cows hadn't come in, so he went out to check and found it laying by the tank with its back broken. He immediately called the base, because he had seen the aircraft flying around the area. They never did find out who killed the cow. When we got ready to leave for basic training, the commandant was out saying good-bye to all the cadets, asking each one of us, "Okay, it's all over now, and it's too late for me to do anything about it. I'm just curious. Who the heck was it? Who killed the cow?" "Sorry, sir. I have no idea." He never found out.

I went to Chico for basic training. When we had completed our training there, they selected cadets from the graduating class to go back to their primary schools and talk to the graduating cadets; give them some information about what to expect when they got to basic. I was selected to go back to King City. My instructor and I jumped in a BT-13, flew down to King City, and landed. Who meets us when we park the airplane but Captain Kelly? He takes us up to his office, and we have a little get acquainted session . . . we talk over what the plans are for the presentations the following morning. Finally, Kelly says, "Don't I remember you?" I says, "Yes, sir. You sure do. I was a cadet here in the J class." He says, "Oh, yeah. By the way, who killed the cow?" I says, "I'm sorry, sir. I have no idea." "Aw, come on. Every cadet in the class knew who it was. You know who it was. Everybody knew who it was, but we were never able to find out. Come on, tell me. Who was it?" "Sorry, sir. I have no idea."

He dropped it. We made our presentation the following morning, went back out, got in the airplane, took off, and headed back for Chico. As we were flying along, my instructor was sitting in the back, playing with the radio, listening to the Sacramento radio station, listening to music, and so forth. All of a sudden, I hear this voice come over the intercom: "I always wondered why they called Anderson 'Cowboy' when he's from Iowa." He immediately knew who it was, but, just like me, he didn't let on. He never let anybody know who killed the cow.

CHARLES A. WATRY
PT-22 student pilot

Unlike other primaries that had a dozen or more security guards, King City had only five. Therefore, four cadets each night supplemented the security system. Armed with a shotgun and driving an old Model A Ford pickup truck, those who drew guard duty would chug among the silent PT-22s, protecting them from the Nazis and Nips. The war was not too intense at King City.

WALT OHLRICH
SNJ student pilot

Training accidents were often more spectacular than lethal. I was following another SNJ at Milton T when I noticed that a student leveled out high, stalled, dug in a wing tip, and cartwheeled for about two hundred feet. When the plane stopped, it was in pieces. The cockpits were sitting on the center section, the aft fuselage was gone, the other wing half gone, and the engine was torn off at the firewall. The main injuries to the student and instructor were sore ears, from banging their heads on each side of the canopy glass.

GREMLINS GUIDE
*Fourth Air Force stateside
safety summary, March
1944*

While on an aerial gunnery mission, F/O De Long, 328th Fighter Group, collided with a tow target, causing damage to the leading edge and bulkhead of the left wing. The pilot was making a 90 degree side approach when he collided with the target. Noting the number of tow target collisions for this month, it seems that the pilots are trying to knock them down instead of shooting them down.

Lt. Holcombe, 328th Fighter Group, forgot to lower his landing gear and made a belly landing, which caused major damage to his airplane. The radio car shot a flare and Lt. Holcombe either did not see it or disregarded it. It appears that Lt. Holcombe was using the wrong form of transportation. A truck might be better for him—it has a fixed landing gear.

Two pilots, 481st Night Fighter Group, were charged with buzzing the Rankin Aeronautical Academy field at Tulare, California, on 4 February 1944, and hedge-hopping along Highway 99 north of Fresno. Both pilots were convicted by general court martial held at Hammer Field on 3 March 1944 and were sentenced to dismissal from the service.

CORNELIA FORT
Women's Auxiliary Ferrying Service pilot, first woman pilot to be killed on active duty (at Laredo, Texas, 21 March 1943)

They chatter about the glamour of flying. Well, any pilot can tell you how "glamorous" it is. We get up in the cold dark in order to get to the airport by daylight. We wear cumbersome flying clothes and a 30 pound parachute. You are either hot or cold; your lipstick wears off, and your hair gets straighter and straighter. You look forward all afternoon to a bath and a steak, and get the bath but rarely the steak. Sometimes you're too tired to even eat. None of us can put into words why we fly. . . . But I know it is dignity, self-sufficiency and pride of skill. I know it is the satisfaction of usefulness.

BUD FURNEY
F4F pilot, VF-4

It was like landing an ice skate. It was said that there were two kinds of Wildcat pilots: those who had ground looped and those who were about to do so. I logged my ground loop at NAS Guantanamo Bay, Cuba, where I went off the runway to the left, dragging the left wing, contrary to usual experience. One of our pilots ground looped a Wildcat to the right and tore up the left wing only to get the airplane righted and go into a ground loop to the left and tear up the right wing! The Wildcat demanded certain expertise and constant attention.

TOMMY BLACKBURN
F4U pilot, VF-17

The flight deck of the *Charger* was some fifty feet wide, and with the long nose of the Corsair pointed up during the approach, all I could see on the final straight part of the approach was "Catwalk" and his paddles out on his platform over the water. On my first try, when he swept his right paddle across his throat at the "cut" signal, I chopped the throttle and abruptly pushed the stick forward. This was a mistake. I got the view of the flight deck ahead that I so desperately wanted, but also set up an ungodly sink rate. I hit on three points with a teeth rattling jolt and bounced up a good twenty feet. Fortunately, or perhaps unfortunately, my arresting hook had picked up an arresting cable and this snapped the plane back down on the deck even harder than that first ferocious impact, blowing out both main tires.

DONALD MARKS
P-40 pilot, fighter transition

The Rube Goldberg gear design required moving the gear handle up and then depressing a button on the stick, which actuated an electric hydraulic motor. About thirty seconds were required for this cycle, and

I came to believe that every P-40 pilot ought to have a third hand. Moreover, the gear rotated ninety degrees as it retracted, and because it was not always symmetrical during the process, the long nose took some fright-inducing wanderings before the gear nestled into the wing wells.

The need to constantly monitor the rudder trim produced its share of victims. Toward the end of the course, and while flying a three-ship formation, the number two man apparently attempted to reset rudder trim while in normal formation. With his head in the cockpit, he fell back but drifted into the lead ship so that lead's empennage suddenly became a flapping, shredded mass of metal and canvas. Amazingly enough, lead managed some degree of control, but elevator action was virtually nonexistent. A hasty airborne conversation resulted in the lead pilot electing to bail out—which he did.

I remember him slowing the aircraft down, sliding back the canopy, carefully stowing the Form 1 in his flight suit, crawling out on the wing root, and sliding down the trailing edge to blossom just before entering a thin, partial undercast. And for what seemed like an eternity, that pilotless P-40 continued in flight before the left wing finally drooped and the machine eventually entered a steep, pseudospiral before vigorously merging with an Alabama peanut field. Thereafter, our lead pilot was, for days, the hero of the base and a man who commanded much awe and respect.

KEITH MATZINGER
B-25 pilot, bomber transition

How do you identify a B-25 pilot? Easy: If he doesn't have a hearing aid, he probably needs one.

DEAN "DIZ" LAIRD
F4F pilot, VF-41

At Norfolk we were ordered to go aboard the USS *Ranger* for combat duty. At 8:00 A.M. the next morning I reported in to fly a Wildcat out to the carrier only to find the bachelor pilots (most of the squadron) trying to recover from a party the night before. One hung-over lieutenant was being held in the cold shower to get him awake enough to fly his Wildcat out to the carrier. Though he didn't seem to be responding, at least he could walk, so they took him out to the line, hauled him up into the cockpit and got him strapped in, then started his fighter and pointed out to sea where the carrier was steaming. This seemed to be acknowledged with what was considered enough intelligence that they let him go. He made it, but once he had caught a wire and come to a stop, he didn't make a move. They had to haul him out, shut down his fighter for him, and put him in the sack. He woke up around 5:00 P.M., remembering nothing after 10:00 P.M. the previous night!

ABOVE *The Grumman TBF Avenger
entered the war at Midway and
served throughout World War II as a
torpedo and attack bomber.* ARNOLD/
NASM

When army bomber pilots left advanced training in small twin-engine ships like the Cessna UC-78 "Bamboo Bomber," they stepped into some big airplanes, such as this Boeing B-17G Flying Fortress flown by Byron Trent, assigned to a bomber transition unit at Hendricks Field, Sebring, Florida, Z.I., or Zone of Interior, as the United States was referred to in official military communications. Though the '17 was initially imposing, it was probably the most docile of all four-engine wartime bombers to fly. By the time the war ended, it had the lowest accident rate of any aircraft built. Pilots found it would fly on two engines without great difficulty . . . as many said, it handled just like a big Piper Cub. BYRON TRENT

A Boeing Stearman N2S Kaydet, the "Yellow Peril," gets an engine change at NAS New Orleans early in the war. NATIONAL ARCHIVES

The pilots at Napier Field, Alabama, remembered this WASP (Women Airforce Service Pilot), sitting in an AT-6, simply as "Buzz." After the initial shock of seeing women flying high-performance fighters and bombers, most pilots accepted them as equals, able to handle everything from a P-51 to a B-29. The initial batch of women assigned to fly military aircraft were in the Women's Auxiliary Ferrying Service (WAFS), which later gave way to the WASPs. Ironically, these women, many of whom were killed during their tours, were never inducted into the armed services and did not receive veterans benefits until more than thirty years after the war's end.

PAUL THOMAS/BOB RICKARD

In the 1930s and early 1940s, the navy taught its fledgling pilots to fly all types of aircraft before getting their wings: floatplanes, flying boats, single-engine fighters, multi-engine patrol bombers. This expensive system was done away with as wartime pressures caught up with reality, yet seaplane pilots, such as this steely-eyed student at NAS Pensacola, were still taught the basics in Naval Aircraft Factory N3N biplanes on floats.

NATIONAL ARCHIVES VIA STAN PIET

When pilots returned from overseas, they were often put straight into a transition unit instructing new pilots on combat technique. After flying a tour in P-40s with the 79th Fighter Group in North Africa, Charles "Jazz" Jaslow came home to instruct in Republic P-47 Thunderbolts at Walterboro, South Carolina. Here he flies a P-47D over Hartford, Connecticut, during the winter of 1944.
CHARLES JASLOW

When the U.S. Army Air Corps established Randolph Field, Texas, as the "West Point of the Air," it rapidly took on an aura of adventure and daring for Depression-era kids, graphically expressed in popular movies such as I Wanted Wings. *These* blue-suited cadets head out across the flight line for their instructors, who stand before individual North American BT-14s with parachutes ready on the wings. FRED E. BAMBERGER, JR.

BELOW *When AAF fighter units got to the point of reaching operational training, they would often go on maneuvers to a bare base and fine-tune tactics, as well as logistics. For P-47 units destined for the Ninth Air Force and support of the coming invasion of Europe, it was more bare than base. In early January 1944, the 406th Fighter Group took its Thunderbolts to Wampee Strip, South Carolina, near Myrtle Beach. The water carrier was about as close to a dining table as several men could find . . . then they had the pleasure of looking forward to sleeping in tents and choking on dust. Brother, it was just a preview of the hardships to come on the Normandy beachhead.* STANLEY J. WYGLENDOWSKI

A North American F-10 on the ramp at Buckley Field, Colorado, March 1945, where pilots and crews learned the basics of photo mapping and reconnaissance work. The F-10 was the camera-equipped version of the famous Mitchell medium bomber, probably the most effective aircraft of its kind of the war. Note the trimetrogon camera fairings under the Plexiglas nose section. Reconnaissance flying was not very glamorous, and pilots often had trouble adjusting to shooting film instead of bullets. In the end, though, they were learning to fly the hottest airplanes in the world, which was the basic reason for enlisting in the first place. OLE C. GRIFFITH

ABOVE *When the Bell P-39 Airacobra proved to be such a disappointment in combat, it was relegated to fighter transition and unit workup in the United States before pilots moved to their assigned type. Light without a full combat load, the '39 proved a delight to fly, giving pilots a good feel for handling a modern fighter. These P-39s await their 406th Fighter Group pilots at Congree, South Carolina, in September 1943 as the group was getting procedures and tactics sorted out before transitioning to P-47s.* JOHN QUINCY VIA STANLEY J. WYGLENDOWSKI

The years before World War II were lean for military aviation, which suffered under the severe budget restrictions of isolationism and the Great Depression. Military pilots were universal in their love for flying, and though many could not stay on active duty, they kept flying in reserve units. These Grumman FF-2s at NAS St. Louis, July 1940, are well beyond *their prime, harking back to the biplane era of aircraft-carrier development. The FF was Grumman's first fighter, the U.S. Navy's first retractable landing gear, closed cockpit aircraft, and the first American fighter to hit 200 mph.* VIA FRED ROOS

Navy patrol bomber pilots became adept at using the Lockheed PV-1 Ventura for high-speed, low-altitude attack work against all kinds of targets, from shipping to air base installations. The airplane, basically a souped-up version of the Lockheed transport series, was a real challenge to fly, particularly if an engine quit on takeoff. But it was fast, real fast, for a bomber in 1943, with twin 2,000-hp engines and light controls, which quickly made for loyal pilots. This PV-1 runs down the California coast during a flight out of the factory field at Burbank. LOCKHEED AIRCRAFT CORP.

RIGHT Saturday afternoon, downtown Headland, Alabama, December 1943. This was the closest thing to civilization near Napier Field during advanced training, so pilots headed down to see the "sights," get a decent meal, and see if any girls were available for Saturday night. Small-town America went through an upheaval thanks to World War II. The outside world forced its way in, and the local girls loved every minute of it.
PAUL THOMAS/BOB RICKARD

Army Air Forces pilots thought there were few more exciting airplanes than the Lockheed P-38 Lightning, a futuristic 400-mph-plus fighter that nudged the sound barrier in a dive, hitting what was then called "compressibility." For anyone who wanted to fly fighters, the Lightning was one of the "hot" ones to ask for. This P-38L, the last model in the line, sits on a stateside ramp awaiting a fortunate pilot. Note the telltale exhaust stains on the booms and vertical fins from the turbosuperchargers which sat on top of each boom near the wing trailing edge. These exhaust-driven turbines gave each Allison engine sea-level carburetor pressure at altitude, a basic operational requirement by 1943. OLE C. GRIFFITH

Though the military services were traditionally a male-only bastion, with wartime came the drastic need for "manpower" in the form of women who weren't going to war. They filled factories, built airplanes, joined all branches of the military, and changed the face of the American work force forever, proving they could do anything asked of them. The army inducted them as WACs (Women's Army Corps), the navy as WAVES (Women Accepted for Volunteer Emergency Service). These WAVES push a combat camouflaged SNJ across the ramp as NAS Jacksonville, Florida. NATIONAL ARCHIVES VIA STAN PIET

A 100-hour inspection being pulled on a North American AT-6D at Napier Field, Alabama, in January 1944. This 600-hp advanced trainer was the first thing student pilots got a hold of that pulled its wheels up, flew like a fighter, and had the "moxie" most were looking for. Without ques- *tion it was one of the most significant aircraft of World War II, because it prepared pilots so well to fly fighters and bombers, though most bomber and transport pilots skipped the AT-6 (SNJ in the navy) to get their wings in multi-engine trainers.* PAUL THOMAS/ BOB RICKARD

Ole C. Griffith climbs up on the wing of his Boeing Stearman PT-17 biplane trainer at Dorr Field, Alabama, in 1943. U.S. Army Air Forces and U.S. Navy primary training was accomplished, for the most part, in open-cockpit biplanes without radios or much instrumentation . . . some felt it might as well have been Dawn Patrol, *because the aircraft appeared to be so antiquated. Yet this heavy, underpowered, ground-looping "washing machine" produced pilots with sharp reflexes and a genuine feel for seat-of-the-pants flying, a basic requirement for flying powerful propeller-driven fighters and bombers.*
OLE C. GRIFFITH

BELOW *When army pilots got their wings, they headed for a transition program of ten hours or so, or were assigned directly to an operational unit and jumped right in. These 33rd Fighter Group pilots sit in the ops shack at Martin State Airport, Baltimore, March 1942, during workups in the Curtiss P-40E. Hastily constructed temporary buildings were thrown up around the country to accommodate the rapidly expanding services. They were drafty, ill equipped, and fire traps, but they allowed people to get the job done.* J. P. CROWDER VIA DOROTHY HELEN CROWDER

Prewar military flying was a world of color, splash, and dash, particularly in the U.S. Navy and Marine Corps. Aircraft were painted in bright color combinations denoting flight leaders, wingmen, squadrons, and a host of other airborne recognition devices. This marine SBD-1 Dauntless of VMB-1 in 1940 would soon lose its plumage in favor of low-visibility, gray-tone camouflage as war approached. An era had passed, along with a nation's innocence. DOUGLAS/ HARRY GANN VIA TOM DOLL

RIGHT *During stateside workups to go aboard the USS* Chenango *for its Pacific combat tour, Ens. Paul D. Thompson forgot to lower his landing gear and put this Grumman TBF Avenger, "Southern Comfort," down on its belly at Otay Mesa, near San Diego. Thompson's shipmates removed the fur collar from an issue leather jacket, glued it to a chamber pot, and awarded it to him for the accomplishment. Training accidents took far more lives and scrapped more aircraft than combat, at a rate of something like five to one. Military flying was a demanding skill, which suffered under the pressure of getting crews into the war zones as fast as possible. A high attrition rate, though horrifying, was accepted as a part of winning the war.* EDWARD W. SIMPSON, JR.

The war effort became a total commitment on the part of most Americans, who, though they often had to do without certain things, were willing to help win it. That included Hollywood, which lost several actors and technicians to the service, including Robert Taylor (right), an experienced pilot who became a flight instructor in the navy. Although he repeatedly requested combat duty, his excellent record caused the pleas to fall on deaf ears. The Vultee SNV-2 Valiant in the background was more commonly known in the army and navy as the "Vibrator," because it made a whale of a racket and seemed to rattle continuously in flight as students went through it during basic flight training. NATIONAL ARCHIVES VIA STAN PIET

LEFT *By 1942 the United States was beginning to catch up in development of top-notch aircraft to replace the obsolete machines it was using just after the attack on Pearl Harbor. There was no more stunning example of this than the Vought F4U Corsair, the first American Navy fighter to top 400 mph in level flight. Its unusual inverted gull wing, powerful 2,000-hp Pratt & Whitney R-2800 engine, and massive Hamilton Standard propeller (all products of United Aircraft) gave navy and marine pilots something to shoot for during training, when instructors seemed to major in yelling and minor in motivation. Here Vought test pilot Willard Boothby prepares to make a factory acceptance flight in a brand new F4U-1.* NASM ARNOLD COLLECTION

LEFT *Goose Bay, Labrador, became a major intermediate point in flying American aircraft across the Atlantic to Europe—and back. The only problem was the forbidding cold and snow, which made airplanes, particularly engines, behave like stubborn mules. Though most of the Martin B-26 Marauders here at Goose are covered with canvas tarps over every possible opening, it still took a preheater, such as the one the ground crew is struggling with, to warm the engines and oil enough to turn over. Nobody fell in love with arctic weather.* MORRIS DAVIDSON, MD VIA RICHARD DAVIDSON, DMD

ABOVE *One of the standard fixtures in making wartime separations bearable was Alberto Vargas's wonderful* Esquire *magazine centerfolds and calendars. They were spread across barracks rooms around the world and became the prime inspiration for the incredible phenomenon of aircraft-nose art. This was Ole Griffith's room during his tour in Peru as an F-10 Mitchell pilot with the 91st Photo Mapping Squadron. Going to sleep at night was a sweet experience . . . or maybe it was frustrating . . . depended on your point of view.* OLE C. GRIFFITH

The Consolidated PB2Y Coronado
production line in San Diego was
covered by camouflage netting
throughout the war as a precaution
against Japanese invasion. NATIONAL
ARCHIVES

TOP RIGHT *Grumman's F6F Hellcat
became the Navy's primary wartime
carrier fighter, claiming more enemy
aircraft than any other shipborne
type.* ARNOLD/NASM

BOTTOM RIGHT *One of the most beloved of all World War II aircraft,
the Consolidated PBY Catalina was
called upon to do everything from
flying torpedo missions at night to
picking up downed aircrew under
fire.* 73RD BOMB WING ASSN. VIA DAVID W.
MENARD

OVER THE HUMP

China-Burma-India

R. T. SMITH
P-40 pilot, Flying Tigers

Compared to the hell that was Rangoon, Kunming was heaven. We were provided with good quarters, decent food, and the climate was invigorating. We shared alert duty with the 1st (Adam & Eve) Squadron, but there was lots of time off, and the Japanese Air Force was suddenly conspicuous by its absence; they had been somewhat rudely surprised on December twentieth when elements of the 1st and 2nd Squadrons, only recently arrived, intercepted ten of their unescorted "Sally" bombers near Kunming and shot down nine of them. Now, after years of indiscriminate and unopposed bombing of Kunming on nearly a daily basis, the Japanese had left this teeming city, the northern terminus of the Burma Road, unmolested for nearly two weeks. The Chinese people were appropriately grateful, and their press began calling us their "Flying Tigers of the sky." Except for a few missionaries, we were about the only Americans in Kunming, and all of us were treated as heroes. Naturally, we ate it up.

JAMES BELLAH
glider infantryman, 1st Air Commando Group

Here we go—packed to the guards—with no power but gravity to bring us in. Here we go into a blind clearing at better than a hundred miles an hour, howling down the night wind, deep in the heart of enemy territory, with a whole Jap army between us and home. Trees—and we're over them! The lights—and they've shot past under us! A long, flat shadowland ahead and we flatten for it, level off, sink toward it, strike it and bounce. The skids tear into it and the dust blots us out, streaming behind us across the clearing like the tail of a meteor. Then suddenly we have swung slightly right and stopped and the doors fly open and the security party is off on the run, fanning out on a perimeter of 360 degrees—moving toward the jungle that is all around us and that may burst into shattering enemy fire at the next breath.

Colorful, graphic nose art came into its own during World War II, expressions of longing far from home or a hot rodder's dream with the ultimate hot rod. The 12th Bomb Group, which had earned its spurs flying B-25s in North Africa, transferred to the CBI with an artist who became known throughout the theater for his outstanding nose art creations. This 82nd Squadron B-25J at Fenny, India (now Bangladesh), has a fanciful bulldog and her pups going off to war with more enthusiasm than skill. No doubt many new crews felt the same way. Because the bulldog was a part of the 82nd's insignia, it featured in much of the unit's nose art.

HANK REDMOND

DON LOPEZ
P-40 pilot, 23rd Fighter Group

Supplies were just terribly tight. You had to have real high priority to get anything over the Hump except ammunition and so on. Madame Chiang Kai-shek was living in the States, and she came back to India with a bunch of real expensive antique furniture pieces she wanted to take to her home in Chung King. Of course, she was able to get it on a C-46 because she had whatever priority she needed, but

25

the pilot was infuriated. He got halfway over the Hump, declared an emergency, and had it all pushed out! Including a piano! When he got close to Kunming, he feathered an engine, so they couldn't do anything to him. He was one of my heroes. I never met him, but I thought he was my kind of person.

CARL FRITSCHE
B-24 pilot, 7th Bomb Group

At Luliang, China, which has an altitude of six thousand feet, I complained bitterly about this practice of overloading. But the situation in the East was critical, so I was given a pat on the shoulder and told to get flying. My plane was already overloaded when I started to taxi out, so when I was flagged down and six fighter pilots climbed aboard I was furious. My gunners had to go to the rear of the plane, causing the plane's tail skid to drag the ground like a ruptured goose. The fighter pilots, a "gung-ho" gang with a lot of energy and chatter, were just in from the States to ferry planes back from the eastern China bases. The flight deck was crawling with people.

Luliang's gravel runway was ten thousand feet long and built high in the mountains. The hundreds of Chinese who maintained the runway had a custom of running across as a plane took off, so that when it passed close behind them, it would cut off the evil spirits they believed followed them. The closer the plane came to them, the more evil spirits were cut off. From a standing start I rammed the throttles forward, released the brakes, and started to roll. The Chinese saw us coming, and huge numbers started running. Several men with water buffalo and carts plodded across and made it just as number 4 prop passed over them. The fighter pilots had never seen anything like this, so they were having the time of their lives.

I wasn't laughing! We were down the field and not near the speed we should have been. The fighter pilots kept laughing and shouted, "Pull'er off into a good chandelle!" As we closed in on the end of the runway, I took a quick look over my shoulder. The chatter had stopped, and all I could see was a bunch of pale-faced pilots with eyes about twice the size they ought to be. My engineer kicked the gear handle when we ran off the ten-thousand-foot runway. As the gear started up, I could feel the plane settle off the end of the runway and into a ravine down the mountain. I had dropped below the level of the runway and the tower kept calling to ask if I was in trouble. Ever so carefully I followed the ravine until I felt secure enough to try to climb. When we were finally out of danger, the fighter pilots were no longer jovial. One of them shook my hand and said, "They ought to give you boys the Distinguished Flying Cross every time you take off in one of these SOBs!"

DON LOPEZ
P-40 pilot, 23rd Fighter Group

India was a garden spot compared to China. Each time we were lucky enough to be assigned the job of ferrying a new fighter back, we'd arrive in Calcutta, buy the commissary out, and gobble up anything else that looked fit to eat. It was unheard of to ferry an empty aircraft back from India, so the next time I went I bought three barracks bags full of food and crammed them into the P-40 from the tail wheel forward by crawling into the fuselage. Each bag was too heavy to lift, so I unloaded them into the fighter, along with my B-4 bag, a new phonograph, and as many records as I could buy.

Once settled in the cockpit, I discovered I couldn't move the stick! Too much food jammed against the control cables. I got out, rearranged the goodies (heaven forbid I leave any of it behind), strapped back in, and taxied out. As the P-40 gathered speed, the tail never came up—the thing went straight up with full forward stick and full nose down trim. Fortunately the Allison was delivering enough power to make the out-of-balance fighter fly back to China. Arriving at Moenbury, I could not get the main gear onto the runway—the tail wheel hit, and the P-40 sailed down the runway with the mains off until she stalled. At least I did better than the guy who loaded eight cases of beer in the left wing of his '51. When he took off he dragged a wing, cartwheeled, got out, and watched the aircraft burn up. Hell, fighter pilots thought C.G. meant commanding general. We hadn't bothered with center of gravity since preflight . . . that was for bomber and transport pilots.

BOB HILLMAN
B-24 pilot, 308th Bomb Group

Next to me in the bar at the Carnarny Estate Hotel in Calcutta there was a C-47 troop-transport pilot with a problem. He had a personally signed requisition from the general who was the chief of supply, CBI, for some ungodly amount of cases of beer. He said, "My problem is that I can't get them all in the C-47. What will I do with these extra two hundred cases of beer?" I said, "I think I've got the answer to your problem."

We took a train back to the base, where we had the engines changed. We flight-checked the aircraft, and then we flew it to Dum-Dum Airport in Calcutta. I had a copy of the requisition in my hand. This fellow was waiting for me, and we loaded those two hundred cases into that B-24. Then going up to twenty-four thousand feet, or whatever it was, we had cold beer for the entire squadron. I thought that was one of the high points of my career.

MILT MILLER
B-24 bombardier, 308th Bomb Group

Doctor James Marshall (name changed to protect the innocent) was perfectly satisfied with his lot as G.P. back home but was thoroughly miserable as a flight surgeon in China. He wanted to fly! He wanted to be in combat and write thrilling stories home about "flak so thick you could float on it" or "there he was coming at me with all guns blazing" or "those bombs walked a line right to the target."

As far as Doc was concerned, he led a dull, uneventful, stupid life diagnosing headaches, dysentery, and the clap. After all those expensive years in medical school, he was reduced to dispensing two brown bombers, two aspirin, or two sulpha tablets.

Being a pilot; that was the life! Or the thrill of finger-tipping the bombsight and hitting a target from eighteen thousand feet. Or handling twin .50-caliber machine guns and watching your tracers eat into a Zero. Or working with the radio. Or navigating a thousand miles out and finding your way back.

Life had dealt Doc a low blow! So Doc hung out with the combat crews and was as solicitous with them as a mama cat with a litter of newborn kittens. The combat cookies were far from dumb. They had Doc pegged, and a shaky hand or a sleepless night was always good for a couple of shots of likker, or a weekend off combat status.

And when a crew, for whatever reason, had to bail out, with Doc lending a sympathetic ear, it was good for at least two weeks in Calcutta on Rest & Relaxation, and if you were really lucky and a good actor, a ticket home. "Doc, we walked all day and all night. No food. No water. And we knew the Japs were back of us. We could hear them. We kept on, past all exhaustion, because we weren't about to be caught! We'd die before we'd let the Japs torture us. Oh, Doc!"

"Grounded until further notice."

"Doc, I have nightmares. I see myself falling, falling, falling, and my chute won't open. I wake up screaming. Help me, Doc, help me. I'm sorry, Doc. But I can't stop crying. The tears just come."

"Section eight. Send him home."

"It hurts when I breathe, Doc. I never told anyone because I want to fly, but when I hit the ground, the wind slammed me into a big rock. I bled from the ears. Don't tell anyone, Doc. Swear! But maybe you can give me a pill to stop the pain in my chest."

"Transferred to the 110th Station Hospital."

And Doc? He was turning into a nervous wreck. He felt like a new father wanting to go through labor pains with his wife. These boys, these heroic boys, were going through hell, and he was still keeping sick-call hours and handing out milk sugar and vitamins.

Finally, Doc talked the squadron commanding officer into letting him fly along on what promised to be a milk run. It was, until an unexpected squadron of Zeros hit them as they were leaving the target. The whole experience up to the point of the Zero attack was Dullsville. In fact, Doc was surprised that most of the crew seemed half-asleep and awoke only to open the bomb-bay doors and drop the bombs.

But things got a little hectic when a lucky string of tracers hit number one engine and it caught fire. The pilot feathered the prop, but now number two engine was acting up. "Get ready to bail out," ordered the pilot. "Everybody line up in the bomb-bay."

To Doc, this was destiny, and he was the first out. His chute opened effortlessly, and he almost glided to a rocking-chair landing in a rice paddy. He noticed the other chutes as he was wafting down, but they disappeared over the hills. No sooner had he landed than he was approached by two peasants who bowed deeply and by sign language urged Doc to follow them. He did, to a small village where he was led to what obviously was the chief's house.

In these primitive surroundings he was treated as a visiting head of state. His shoes were shined. He was wined and dined with the best these poor people had to offer. And the local philharmonic consisting of a tree-trunk drum, a triangle, two sticks, and cymbals played Moo Chu's Symphony no. Six in L-Flat Minor. Doc was touched and thrilled with the hospitality.

The next two or three hours passed like minutes, and it was with obvious regret that it was made plain to Doc that it was time to move on. The triple-distilled rose-petal wine Doc had been slugging down was having its effect, and he was just too happy with his new friends to want to leave them. There were tears as Doc accepted a pair of embroidered slippers, two ounces of opium gum, a broken compass, and a bottle of jing bao juice as farewell gifts. He reluctantly refused the offer of the chief's twin sixteen-year-old daughters.

Doc started to walk down the path after his guide, but to his amazement he was hoisted onto the back of the local strong man. It would be a loss of face to allow such a distinguished visitor to walk! So the procession—really, an entourage—accompanied by the Tympany Four started on the way to Kunming.

Of course there was a stop at each farmhouse, where protocol dictated that Doc imbibe some more wine and sweets, and by the time they reached the river, Doc couldn't walk if he had wanted to. A boat was waiting and the strong current and adept oarsmen sped the craft downriver while Doc lolled on a bamboo seat eating peanuts and tangerines.

The first night was spent at a Buddhist temple. Although the comforts were meager, Doc had no trouble falling asleep on a flat board atop two sawhorses, with a cotton quilt over the wood to minimize splinter damage. The next morning found an entirely new group to lead the way, and although Doc had little time to meet or socialize with his hosts at the temple, he was showered with gifts, including an ancient carbine and a beautiful silk robe.

There was a lavish breakfast, simply delicious, and a pinkish wine with the kick of a tiger. Again, fond farewells, and "don't forget to write" and "be sure to call if you get to town" and "see you all next year."

This time Doc traveled in style. No more piggy back. He had the local mandarin's sedan chair. So off they went with cymbals clanging to ward off evil spirits and drums beating an exotic code to inform the countryside that an important personage was passing through. There were, of course, frequent stops at farmhouses and villages, where the proper amenities were observed and gifts given.

Doc was convinced that he needed only two more days of collecting loot and he'd have enough goodies to open the biggest boutique in Kunming. Late in the afternoon, they reached the capital of the province, and the entourage became a mad, mad parade. The sedan chair was held high and carried by eight strong men down the main street with banners strung from poles, flowers lining the way, and firecrackers celebrating the occasion. Cheering crowds lined the curbs.

Doc was brought to the governor's palace, where the muck-a-mucks of the province were already seated in the vast banquet hall. The sedan chair was carried in, and Doc was softly deposited in the seat of honor. At last there was someone who spoke English and who informed Doc that he was being honored as the representative of all the brave Americans who had come to China to fight the evil Japanese.

Doc responded with an inspired speech—slurry due to a slight case of imbibitis—and his words were translated to a wildly cheering audience. There was eating and drinking and entertainment by acrobats, magicians, and singers. It was really quite an evening. Doc was king of the roost, and he was ready to let it continue forever.

However, all good things must end, and bright and early the next morning a B-25 landed on the short strip to take Doc back home. As the plane took off and Doc realized that he was flying back to his home base, a tear rolled down his cheek. It was really a pleasure to bail out if one was to be left with memories such as those Doc would be able to relish the rest of his life. But back to harsh reality!

The rest of the crew was coming in from the bailout and needed medical attention. First was the pilot. "It's my back, Doc. It's killing me. I practically had to crawl all the way home. I can't straighten up."

"Two aspirin. Next."

"I hit my head on a rock. There's a ringing in my ears and I keep seeing stars. I've also blacked out once or twice this morning."

"Castor oil. Next."

"What's that on your shoulder, Doc? Tell it to go away! Now there's two of them. Watch out, Doc, they're eating your left ear!"

"See the chaplain. Next."

And so it went. No longer was Doc the patsy of the squadron. He had bailed out, and as far as he was concerned, the experience was worth another tour of duty. Good idea! He'd have to recommend it to the Group Commanding Officer.

DON LOPEZ
P-51 pilot, 23rd Fighter Group

We made some pretty unusual "cargo" flights with our fighters from China to India and back. Often only one fuel tank was filled in India so that the other could be poured full of booze. We had to make sure the lineman at home base didn't put gas in the important tank before the precious cargo could be drained.

BELOW *The most successful medium bomber of the war, the North American B-25 Mitchell, could do just about any job assigned, from the Doolittle Raiders flying off an aircraft carrier to bomb Tokyo to very low level strafing. This B-25H (armed with 75-mm cannon) of the 491st Squadron, 341st Bomb Group, is running up prior to takeoff at Yankai, China, in the spring of 1945 for a low-level bombing mission. Though the massive artillery piece sounded like a good idea, it was inaccurate and hard to operate because the engineer had to manually load each round before the pilot fired it. These guys came out of the war with very little hearing left.*

CARROLL S. BARNWELL

MIDDLE RIGHT *A 1st Air Commando Group B-25H returning from a mission over Burma, 1944. Finding one's way around over the trackless Asian jungle was an art . . . finding targets was even more so. To boot, there was very little in the way of fresh food or basic comfort due to the need to carry only the most essential items over the Hump. Though crews often felt they were forgotten and neglected, they did their jobs with an enthusiasm many simply pulled out of their hidden reserves. Certainly esprit de corps could be found in common misery and risk if nothing else.*

R. T. SMITH

TOP LEFT *Flying Tiger ace R. T. Smith on patrol over the China-Burma border, May 1942, in one of the one hundred Curtiss Hawk export fighters seconded and sold to China instead of Britain from January through March 1941. Although popular writing about the AVG has always referred to these aircraft as P-40s, technically they were Hawk H81-A2s with four .30-caliber wing guns and two .50-caliber machine guns in the nose. Not as maneuverable as their Japanese adversaries, they were more rugged, carried more firepower, and could outdive just about anything. Pilots were paid from $600 to $750 per month, plus expenses, $30 a month for rations, and a bonus of $500 for each Japanese plane shot down.* R. T. SMITH

BOTTOM LEFT *The very capable Douglas C-54 Skymaster did a great deal to speed operations over the Hump during the last part of the war. This C-54 runs up just before takeoff at Mytkina, Burma, in front of a C-46. Four engines made a tremendous amount of difference in getting over the Himalayas safely, and the '54 was easier to fly than the tailwheel twin-engine types, which had anemic single-engine performance with a load and devastating crosswind problems.* GEORGE SAYLOR VIA BILL BIELAUSKAS

The China-Burma-India Theater of Operations (CBI) was the end of the earth on the logistics pipeline. Everything, from fuel to food to beer to bulldozers, had to be flown over the "Hump," the massive Himalayan mountain range that stretched from Assam, India, to Kunming, China. Overloaded Army Air Forces transports fought some of the worst weather in the world, hanging on their props to clear peaks from 18,000 to 22,000 feet. Between April 1942 and the end of the war, 450 aircraft went down, a steep price to pay for delivering a grand total of 650,000 tons of supplies. This C-47, once finished with its Air Transport Command flying over the Hump, was converted into what appears to be a radio-relay aircraft for XXI Bomber Command's B-29s, which flew into Japan from China starting in June 1944. GEORGE MCKAY VIA LARRY DAVIS

TOP RIGHT Among the first American pilots and ground crews into action in the Far East were Claire Chennault's American Volunteer Group, the Flying Tigers, including former Air Corps flight instructor R. T. Smith, here at Kunming with fellow ace Chuck Older's Hawk 81-A2, an export P-40 originally intended for the British. Through Chennault's brilliant slash-and-dive tactics, the AVG managed to rack up a continual string of kills over superior numbers with a supposedly obsolete fighter

under some of the most difficult conditions imaginable. The entire organization was made up of personnel who left their regular service commissions to fight for China, and when the organization disbanded on 4 July 1942, the U.S. armed services were not all that happy to welcome them back. The stylized winged tiger on the sides of the aircraft was designed by Walt Disney Studios, and the red angel denoted Hell's Angels, the AVG 3rd Pursuit Squadron. R. T. SMITH

When war came to even the most re-mote areas of the world, cultures col-lided as old world met new, both often having to combine methods to get the job done. Though this 10th Combat Cargo Squadron C-47 brought sup-plies to Chanye, China, in December 1944, it took Chinese troops and their horses to get the matériel moved to the front lines. Airplanes were certainly the future personified, yet the horse remained vital in the CBI if the war was to be carried to the enemy. CALVIN BANNON VIA BILL BIELAUSKAS

Capt. Milton M. Molakides, navigator/bombardier with the 341st Bomb Group's 491st Squadron, sits in the pilot's seat of the B-25J he was assigned to. There is no doubt about how much the side pack .50-caliber machine guns have been fired . . . Mitchells were superb strafers, with each model carrying a successively larger complement of guns. The added metal patch under the muzzle of the lower gun did not completely solve the problem of buckling the skin when the guns were fired. Eventually the structure had to be beefed up on the production line. CARROLL S. BARNWELL

TOP RIGHT *An entire series of 12th Bomb Group Mitchells featured the fierce face pictured here on this 82nd Squadron B-25H armed with 75-mm cannon, "Vikin's Vicious Virgin." By far the most popular subject of nose art was the female form, in all manner of dress or undress, profane or sacred, from prostitutes to a reverent vision of "Ave Maria." Squadron commanders often tried to censor these typically American expressions, but the farther from the Z.I. the unit, the more crews seemed to get away with.* HANK REDMOND

BOTTOM RIGHT *"Gooney Birds," C-47s of the 10th Squadron, 3rd Combat Cargo Group, offload at Kutkai airstrip, Burma, near the Chinese border. When the Burma Road was cut off by the Japanese in early 1942, the only alternative was creation of an air line to keep the Allied war effort in China and Burma going. The Hump became a very hazardous proposition, but an average of 700 tons a month got through, first under the Tenth Air Force, then the AAF Air Transport Command, with a record total of 71,042 tons being hauled in July 1945. Toward the end of the war, each day an average of 650 aircraft crossed the Himalayas.* CALVIN BANNON VIA BILL BIELAUSKAS

Navigator Hank Redmond's tent at Monywa, Burma, 1944. "We used to fly from Fenny, India, into Monywa (at that time the enemy lines were only 30 miles away) in an unarmed AT-6 or single B-25 several times to get our targets for the next day's mission just before the fall of Mandalay. That city certainly did not look like anything that Rudyard Kipling wrote about! The British 14th Army would name the targets they needed to be bombed or strafed, then supply whatever photos or detailed maps they might have. Often we would stay overnight in tents like this, then fly back to Fenny where operations and intelligence would prepare our targets for the next morning." HANK REDMOND

BOTTOM RIGHT Ready for the boneyard. After the 12th Bomb Group's "Incendiary Blonde" bellied in at Fenny, India, there wasn't much more anyone could do with her than cart her carcass off to salvage. Navigator Hank Redmond (right), in spite of the hazards of combat and the CBI living conditions, never regretted going to India: "I am grateful to the B-25 as most of my classmates in navigation school were killed in B-17s or B-24s in Europe and B-29s over Japan. Well over half of my graduating class was killed less than 90 days after they left for overseas duty . . . only two of us out of 26 survived the war." HANK REDMOND

A 491st Squadron, 341st Bomb Group B-25H climbs out from Yankai, China, on the wing of another Mitchell, heading for Japanese targets, December 1944. The sun's glare has caught the reflection of the waist gunner's .50-caliber machine gun feed belts. The B-25 was one of the easiest of AAF bombers to fly and operate . . . from pilots to engineers to ground crews there were few complaints, particularly in its ability to absorb battle damage. In the rough field conditions of China and India, the B-25 was a godsend. CARROLL S. BARNWELL

When going into Calcutta for diversion, one never knew what would come into view. Though there were motor vehicles, the basic system of moving anything was manpower. These men seem to be having no trouble at all moving a piano down one of the main streets. HANK REDMOND

TOP RIGHT *This former 1st Air Commando Group P-47 Thunderbolt on the field at Fenny, India, was used by AAF Colonel Schmidt, the American liaison officer with the British Army at Monywa, Burma. As 12th Bomb Group navigator Hank Redmond recalled, "He used his P-47 to help scout out targets that needed air strikes and occasionally would go after some of them by himself if the need was urgent or if he could do the necessary job. He and British 14th Army would select our targets for B-25 strikes. He was a rugged man who did a great job. I don't feel he ever received full credit for his fine work as a loner in this remote location."* HANK REDMOND

BOTTOM RIGHT *Many nations in the Allied coalition fighting the Axis depended on American support to do their part. The Chinese-American Combat Wing (CACW) was comprised of pilots from both nations flying American aircraft, from P-40s to the latest Mustangs, such as this P-51D at Nanking, originally assigned to the AAF 51st Fighter Group before being passed on to the CACW. Officially a Chinese Air Force unit with the national blue-and-white roundel, the Wing flew B-25s as well as fighters in several squadrons. By the end of the war, eight pilots had earned ace status.* GEORGE MCKAY VIA LARRY DAVIS

When they went off to war, most Americans had barely been off the farm. Within a very short time they were living and working in exotic locales, straight out of the storybooks. When Cal Bannon, 10th Combat Cargo Squadron, went on leave in Calcutta, March 1945, he was captivated by the bustling city and its policemen, who did such a colorful job of directing traffic. CALVIN BANNON

TOP RIGHT *"Satan's Daughter," a 10th Combat Cargo Squadron C-47, was flown by Lts. Herman Witten and Jake Saylor from Florida to India, where they flew her in service over some of the roughest terrain in the world . . . and through some of the roughest weather. Note the extensive fog below—and the load master doesn't seem to be too concerned about falling out. It was a different kind of war in a different kind of world.*
GEORGE SAYLOR VIA BILL BIELAUSKAS

BOTTOM RIGHT *When Hank Redmond, 12th Bomb Group, got to Calcutta, he thought it "was one of the filthiest cities in the world . . . no one seemed to be working at the time. The city smelled bad even at 5,000 feet . . . you could smell the odor from sewage, the dead and just the city." Nevertheless, he was fascinated by things, such as this Sikh driving a vintage taxi through downtown at breakneck speed.* HANK REDMOND

41   *Over the Hump*

WHAT SOFT UNDERBELLY?

The Mediterranean

JEEP CROWDER
P-40 pilot, 33rd Fighter Group

11 NOV. '42: [North Africa] Jones's engine cut out after he made a left turn and he went down with the ship. He had a premonition about the ship before he boarded the carrier. The group lost 22 airplanes by accident on this landing field. Horton's plane went over on its back and Horton got a broken back.

12 NOV. '42: Slept from 12:30 to 3:15 last night, nearly froze. Back is stiff and have headache from sleeping on concrete with only cover being a raincoat. There are a lot of obsolete bombers here. A C-47 came in today and sure looked good. The food is canned rations. Tonight the lights came on in the hangar and we all write letters home. The French have a lot of junk around here.

25 NOV. '42: Up 6:15 A.M. Been married 9 mo. Hope Baby gets the roses. French check out and do aerobatics in P-40s.

27 NOV. '42: Weather bad. French cracks up P-36. French are good pilots; very spectacular.

7 DEC. '42: Saw Pearl Harbor losses yesterday. Was astonished. Have changed mind about French pilots. They have cracked up 2 P-36s and 2 P-40s.

13 DEC. '42: Have attack mission this afternoon. Group is always frustrating our plans. Our two best planes are sitting out in front prepared for XC and have been waiting there since yesterday. Our attack mission is called off, and we are supposed to put on a show using 16 planes for some general even tho we have to stop patrols to do it. I'm beginning to think this is a political war in this part of the country.

25 DEC. '42: Up 9 A.M. Been married 10 mo. Went down town as part of delegation to invite American nurses to Xmas Party. Beggs dropped 14 bottles of wine and busted it. We went down and bought some more after much argument. Party started at 5:30 P.M. and lasted until 11 P.M. Lots of guys got drunk; I didn't but I don't know why. I sure was lonesome in spite of all the spirits. To bed a very lonely fellow at 12MN.

RALPH "DOC" WATSON
P-38 pilot, 14th Fighter Group

19 NOVEMBER 1942: Today was more interesting for some boys. Col. Olds and 12 went as escort to 6 B-17s to Tunis. Zeigler had a good shot at a 109 but pressed the mike button instead of the gun button.

When the AAF finally moved onto the boot of Italy, accommodations became somewhat more permanent, though tents were replaced by shacks built from belly-tank crates. These 37th Squadron, 14th Fighter Group pilots (Lieutenants Chuck Leonard, Krug, unknown, John Jones, McHaug, Anderson) are on their way out of the ops building at Triolo, Italy, under a sign that seems to have been a permanent part of flying fighters in every war. The sunglasses were invented by Bausch & Lomb for the AAF under a spec requiring 97 percent UV filtration. They have been Ray Bans ever since. The helmet is RAF issue, much superior in comfort, noise protection, and durability to American helmets. Pilots secured them whenever they could pull off some form of trade.
JAMES STITT

43

KEN KAILEY
*C-47 pilot, 8th Troop
Carrier Squadron*

We quite often flew with one of the cargo doors removed on short-haul freight runs. One day, about the time we were leveling off at cruising altitude, the crew chief came forward to tell me we had forgotten to bring in the steps. They were still hanging outside the plane. So I asked the co-pilot to go back and help the crew chief and radio operator to try and bring the steps in—to avoid returning to the field. I later found out that their idea of "help" was to hold the co-pilot by the ankles while he lay belly down with his head in the slipstream and struggled with the steps. Just about the time they succeeded in bringing in the steps, the right engine quit. I think that co-pilot must have set a world's record for the standing broad jump. He made it from the back door up into the cockpit in the few seconds it took to switch tanks—standing alongside asking, "Wha' hoppen?" and ready to help.

BUD ABBOT
*B-17 pilot, 483rd Bomb
Group*

There was one mission to Budapest when we got hit. We didn't lose anybody on the crew, but flak destroyed the radio room. The wall between it and the bomb bay was gone, the radios were all shot, the floor was about half-destroyed, and Lou LaWicky, the radio operator, was hanging sort of half in and half out of the airplane. The waist gunners grabbed him and pulled him back in and laid him on the floor back in the waist. His table probably saved his life, because he got all of the flak in the lower part of his legs.

After they released the other bomb that was stuck, the right wing tank had a big split in the seam, leaking gas and burning. The ball-turret gunner, our armaments man, went into the bomb bay with a fire extinguisher, held it up against the seam, and put the fire out.

There were gasoline fumes throughout the airplane, particularly in the waist area. LaWicky didn't lose consciousness, and he kept asking for a cigarette. All the guys said, "We can't give you the cigarette. If we light a match, we'll all go down!" Since they couldn't give him a cigarette, somebody said, "Let's find the first-aid kit and give him a shot of morphine; get him calmed down." They couldn't find the first-aid kit. Searched and searched and searched; never could find the first-aid kit.

All the way back, of course, we had to let down, scared we were going to have to jump. One of the B-17s out of the formation came down with us for a while, then he went on. We couldn't mess with the controls. We were afraid to. We started discussing: "Okay, now, what's going to happen? Are we going to be able to make it all the way back? Maybe we should bail out; abandon this thing." Two of us kept saying, "No, no. If we bail out, LaWicky won't make it, so, as long as this airplane will fly, let's stay with it." We threw out the guns and the ammo and everything that we could grab to lighten the ship. All four engines ran okay.

Finally, we were back, approaching the Adriatic coast over Yugoslavia. Somebody said, "Well, now, it's iffy. What if we go down in the Adriatic? We're all going to die. We ought to bail out over Yugoslavia. We'll get picked up and we can get back to base." I said, "No, let's stick with the airplane." So we did . . . crossed the Adriatic, got over the hills just after. We agreed, "Okay, instead of going back to our base, let's go to Foggia-Main, because they've got a concrete runway, and that's where all the major maintenance facilities are, and the hospital's right there." So we went right on in to Foggia-Main. We had no radio, so we shot a red flare, and they gave us a green flare, telling us to come on in and land.

We had no hydraulic system, so we cranked the gear down. Then somebody said, "What are we going to do? We've got no brakes." The bombardier got on the intercom, "I'll take care of that." He took two waist parachutes and fastened them to the gun mounts over the two waist guns, then said, "As soon as we touch down, release those two chutes."

They did. One of them billowed out okay; the other one didn't, but it helped to slow us down. We kind of ground looped, then came to a stop. Of course, we were swarmed on immediately by all the emergency vehicles. The ambulances and doctors were there, and they took Lou out in a stretcher, put him in an ambulance, and off to the hospital. He eventually lost his legs. I think three other guys had minor flesh wounds . . . they treated them right there and released them.

When I got out of the airplane I had my kit bag in one hand, helmet in the other, and they had to pry my hands open to get me to let loose of them. I was cool, calm, and collected the whole time, until we landed that airplane and I got off it. I think everybody was in shock. It was something.

JEEP CROWDER
P-40 pilot, 33rd Fighter Group

15 JAN. '43: I was sitting on alert over in front of 58th, when three FW 190s came over and dropped bombs about 100yds to the left of the nose of plane. Then they and 2 Me 109s ground strafed us. It took 10 years off my life. One of them shot "Wild Horse" Watkins down, he parachuted down and fell backwards, crushing his skull and dying later in the afternoon.

7 APR. '43: Tonight Lt. Gen. Spaatz and Maj. Gen. Doolittle pass out awards in group operations. I get an air medal ribbon; a puny looking thing.

HENRI HENRIOD
intelligence officer, 86th Fighter Bomber Group

The A-36 was a modified P-51, with air brakes to slow the plane in a dive on a target below. It had an air scoop on the bottom, which, intended or not, produced a terrifying whistling, screaming sound that added to its nicknames of Mustang and Invader. The more popular appellation, prompted by the enemy, in whom it put the fear of God, was "Screaming Demons." One had to see and hear it to believe it.

The only water for showering [in North Africa] was salt water, which left one's hair sticky and impossible to comb, and made washing clothes impossible. The flies were multitudinous, as were mosquitoes, requiring netting for us to sleep. Electric lights were unheard of, but hardly necessary, since it was light until bedtime at 9:00 P.M. While marking time, everyone saw the countryside, the paradox that hunger prevailed in a land where, in May, there were vineyards for miles around, plus olive trees, almond trees, and grain.

The squadron's tent city was the pride of the area, with double-deck bunks and drainage trenches. One ingenious group had plumbing fixtures ala GI can, blow torch tradition. Even so, the water still was unpalatable, leading one sergeant to write home to the effect that it tasted like someone already had drunk it.

A few seemed to have suffered slight brain damage. One wrote and told his mother that the mosquitoes were so big, they had poured forty gallons of gas into one of them before they discovered it wasn't one of our planes. Another aberration appeared again in another letter which advised the people at home that it was so hot that "the river got out of its bed, got in the shade of a tree, and just sweated it out."

KEN KAILEY
C-47 pilot, 8th Troop
Carrier Squadron

We had a pilot named James Purcell in the squadron that was affectionately known as a "wild character" (or maybe a "crazy bastard"). Today, he would be called a "free spirit." Somewhere in North Africa he managed to acquire a couple of German motorcycles, and was having a great time roaring about the countryside. Unfortunately, the group commander found out about it and made Purcell get rid of them. It wasn't that the colonel was all that fond of Jim, but pilots were in very short supply right then in troop carrier, and he did not want to lose one.

When the squadron was flying in and out of the Anzio beachhead, the recommended procedure was to approach from the sea for a landing. If you flew too far inland, to approach toward the sea, the pattern could take you out over the lines and the German riflemen would take potshots at you on the base leg. One day, Purcell had some time to waste while waiting for his return flight, so [he] decided to see some of this shooting war. He talked a couple of infantrymen into taking him sightseeing in their jeep. They had gotten pretty close to the lines, and got out to look around. About then, some German soldiers stepped out of the bushes, arms in the air, Kamerad, the whole surrender bit. As Purcell was clawing to get his .45 out of its holster, it went off, and he shot himself in the butt.

The next day, as he lay on the cot in the field hospital, they came around passing out Purple Hearts. Jim graciously declined. But the worst part came when he was evacuated by one of our own squadron planes. You can imagine the sympathy and razzing he received.

RICHARD TOMLINSON
P-38 pilot, 14th Fighter
Group

Until the fall of 1944, we lived in GI tents with no windows, no heat, and, in most cases, no floors. Some had put bricks on the ground for floors. That fall we built the stone houses that are in the pictures you have. We secured the stones for the walls by driving around the countryside, locating stone fences, which we were able to push over because of the old, poor quality mortar. We just helped ourselves to the stones. The roofs were made of belly tank crates and old tent canvas. The window frames, doors, and furniture from old crates of various kinds. The floors were brick, which we bought from a local brickyard and were laid on the ground in the manner that people now make patios.

An enterprising squadron welder made heating stoves from parts of fifty-five-gallon drums, gun heaters from salvaged aircraft and such other hardware items as he could scrounge. Since we had no kerosene or heating oil, we burned 100-octane aviation gas in them. This was very volatile, and accidents happened. On 30 November 1944, when we were moving into our house, I became the first, but not the last, casualty of the heating stoves. My hands were badly burned when the gas exploded as I was lighting the stove. I was out of circulation for three weeks as a result.

DENNIS MCCLENDON
C-47 pilot, 51st Troop Carrier Wing

Our own good old trigger-happy navy was at it again. Johnny Blalock's reaction came instantaneously. He turned right, into the echelon, to keep from angling the formation over the ship and into the barrage balloon. But a right turn into a left echelon is pure murder, especially to my number four ship on the slow inside of the turn.

Violently I wrenched 381 to the right, barely avoiding a collision with Lt. Jimmy Hayes, who was flying number three directly in front, and I chopped the throttles to keep from overrunning him. There was nothing left to do. At 250 feet we had no room for maneuvering. The old plane shivered and shook but she held on. . . . With no power in a 60-degree bank, old 381 could have stalled out at 85 mph and spun in but she didn't. . . .

Ka-flooey, up came those red lines of light again! Slam, bam, we went—up on our right wing tips again. This time it was just too sudden for us. I never knew where the others went, but Grad and I broke off violently. Jimmy's plane was about to come through my cockpit, and closing fast, when I dumped the nose with all my strength and skimmed under the other planes and gliders at full throttle. It was enough to make an atheist pray.

Coming out, we were less than one hundred feet above the water. How Sgt. Evans kept his glider behind us I'll never know. What prevented a tangled mess of four planes and four gliders is a mystery.

KENTON MCFARLAND
B-24 pilot, 93rd Bomb Group

Streaming over Pitesti [Ploești], we're right on schedule, radio silence is still intact, and we're down to less than five hundred feet, low to duck in under the German radar. It's like a Mack Sennett movie all the way. Farm couples down on their knees to pray. Kids toss rocks at us. Horses bolt, overturning wagons full of families. A gal bathing nude in a river almost pulls the entire outfit off course. My men are now talking and joking nervously over the intercom. As we get closer to Ploesti, though, the idle chatter dies away.

Suddenly the 376th is turning right, following a railroad spur. We're boxed in, so we wing over gently and slide back into formation. Mordovancy, my new navigator (four former navigators had been mortally wounded by flak fragments over Italy), up front in the nose, clicks on his intercom and says simply, "I think we turned too soon."

The knot in my stomach's getting even tighter. Polka dots of flak burst in a row above us, and fragments splatter like hail off the ship. I pull in my neck instinctively and drop the plane another fifty feet. The whole squadron seems to hug the ground just a little bit harder with every splatter of flak. In the waists, the guys are opening up at the flak pits. It's like a cow-town fight at close quarters now, instead of the impersonal combat at twenty thousand feet that we're used to.

The western desert of North Africa was a rugged place for Ninth Air Force pilots to get their first taste of combat in the fall of 1942. Blazing during the day, freezing at night, this was a hostile place with a sky full of experienced Luftwaffe pilots who had been at war for three years. Charles "Jazz" Jaslow flew "Sweet Bets," a Merlin-engined P-40F, with the 87th Squadron, 79th Fighter Group. The RAF paint scheme of dark earth, middlestone, and azure blue was typical of many P-40s off the line at Curtiss and ideal for the area. The 87th Squadron insignia, the Skeeters, is painted on the side of the cowling, where crew chief R. Randall is working on a maintenance squawk.

CHARLES JASLOW

Cruising over North Africa . . . a P-40L Warhawk of the 59th Squadron, 33rd Fighter Group, early 1943. The group flew its fighters off the aircraft carrier USS Chenango *as a part of Operation Torch, then set up bare-base operations in French Morocco. The large American flag painted on the side was one of many attempts to identify American planes to the Vichy French defenders, implying the invasion was an all-American operation. The French had little love for the British, so the Allied strategy was to play down their participation.* J. P. CROWDER VIA DOROTHY HELEN CROWDER

LEFT *Loaded with five-hundred-pound bombs, a 524th Squadron A-36A Invader, 27th Fighter Bomber Group, passes Mt. Etna, Sicily, on the way to a target in the fall of 1943. The A-36 was the Allison-engine, dive-bomber version of the P-51 Mustang. It looked so much like the Messerschmitt 109 that yellow stripes were painted on the wings to help Allied gunners and pilots distinguish between the two. The Invader did a fine job, but there weren't enough built, so attrition and general lack of spares took their toll quickly. Dive brakes were fitted on the upper and lower surfaces of the wings, but the pilots generally preferred to have them wired shut.* J. P. CROWDER VIA DOROTHY HELEN CROWDER

BOTTOM LEFT *Home sweet home for "Jeep" Crowder and his fellow 59th Fighter Squadron pilots at Thelepte in the Tunisian desert, early 1943. Sand became a part of everything, including the food. Once in the engine oil, it neatly scoured the inside until tolerances were shot . . . getting new engines was close to miraculous, so ground crews kept them running by any number of unapproved methods.*

The same thing happened with the guns . . . the bores became so smooth that the .50-caliber rounds simply tumbled out. Getting sleep became an art, particularly when the Germans would send nuisance night raids. Although some managed a hit, the bombing didn't work very well. The main idea was to keep everyone awake . . . that worked. J. P. CROWDER VIA DOROTHY HELEN CROWDER

RIGHT *Outdoor maintenance, Foggia, Italy . . . no one's idea of how to run a war, but who said war was convenient? The massive complex of Fifteenth Air Force bomber and fighter bases running from Termoli to Foggia and Cerignola, then down to Brindisi, dominated the eastern coast and heel of the Italian boot. Seven fighter groups (P-38s and P-51s) covering nineteen heavy bomb groups (B-17s and B-24s) could be unleashed on any given day to hit German targets all the way into central Europe. By 1944 the U.S. Army Air Forces was airpower personified across the globe.* USAF

There were no closer ties than those between a pilot and his crew chief . . . and, yet, none more distant. The severe separation between enlisted men and officers created a barrier some managed to overcome but most did not. Pilots knew, without a doubt, their lives were in the hands of their ground crews, so they had a respect that overcame artificial barriers. The ground crews desperately wanted everything to go perfect with "their" airplane, which was usually considered on loan to the pilot. Many pilots treated these non-coms with respect, but many did not. It was a crazy world, in a crazy war, but men, like pilot Lieutenant Honeycutt and crew chief Technical Sergeant Jackson of the 37th Squadron, 14th Fighter Group at Triolo, formed bonds rarely broken. JAMES STITT

A 37th Fighter Squadron P-38 at Triolo, Italy, with nose art inspired by the Alberto Vargas April 1943 Esquire *magazine gatefold. The creations of this man, along with George Petty, caused crews to fill up blank space on thousands of wartime aircraft . . . some were outstanding, some weren't, but the idea was the same. Crews felt the need to personalize their weapons of war as much for luck as for young bravado.* JAMES STITT

Chuck O'Mahony looks down from the cockpit of his stunning "Miss Manchester," a 320th Bomb Group B-26 Marauder that flew out of Sardinia and Corsica in 1944. The unit's nose art was among the more striking in the theater, from shark mouths to beautiful pinups. The mission tally on the side is indicative of the success the 320th had in combat, typical of most Marauder units. It was not unusual to see some pass the two-hundred-mission mark. JOSEPH S. KINGSBURY

A 320th Bomb Group Marauder on the way to a target over southern Italy. When the first B-26s entered service, they gained a bad reputation for being killers, and pilots were fearful of flying them. The aircraft had a smaller wing, which gave it both a high top speed and a higher landing speed. Pilots used to landing at slower speeds were stalling out and crashing. With a little reeducation from pilots such as Jimmy Doolittle, pilots stuck to the "book" speeds and the accidents stopped, giving the Marauder the lowest overall combat-loss rate of any American aircraft.

JOSEPH S. KINGSBURY

BOTTOM RIGHT *Mud, mud, and more mud . . . one of the primary enemies in Italy, as this 37th Fighter Squadron pilot is finding out at Triolo in late 1944. Certainly many problems were solved by the pierced-steel planking (PSP or Marston Matting) here . . . you didn't sink into the mud. However, it created a new set of headaches: the mud oozed through the holes to create a slimy mess, akin to walking on ice with bare feet. Taxiing was one thing, but landing on it beat any ride at Coney Island, with the pilot merely a passenger until everything wound down to a stop.*

JAMES STITT

A 37th Squadron P-38 just about to touch down at Triolo, Italy, home of the 14th Fighter Group, 1944. The Lightning, one of the AAF's three primary fighters, was universally loved by pilots in the Mediterranean, particularly for its firepower and ability to come home on one engine. Big, it had its shortcomings, with no cockpit heat and poor visibility downward, but pilots usually fought to its advantages and tried to minimize its disadvantages. No doubt, though . . . it sure looked hot. JAMES STITT

ABOVE *A 47th Bomb Group Douglas A-20G Havoc lifts off at Malignano Airfield, Sienna, Italy, 1945. The 47th was the only light bomb group assigned to the Twelfth Air Force, which had been fighting its way from Africa ever since Operation Torch in November 1942. The Twelfth was the AAF's tactical air arm in the Mediterranean, particularly after the Fifteenth Air Force was formed, taking the Twelfth's P-38s and B-17s, and the Ninth Air Force moved up to the European Theater. Specializing in close air support, interdiction, and supply work to help move troops on the ground, A-20s, B-25s, B-26s, P-47s, F-5s, F-6s, and C-47s did a fantastic job in the face of strong opposition with very little publicity.* ROBERT R. FRIZELL VIA KENNETH I. KAILEY

TOP RIGHT *The 320th Bomb Group on the way out of Corsica to a target in the Mediterranean, late 1944. The speed and hitting power of the Marauder quickly established it as a valuable medium bomber. A pilot's airplane, it was in many ways like flying a big fighter that carried bombs, not to mention a raft of .50-caliber machine guns, both forward firing and turret operated.* JOSEPH S. KINGSBURY

BOTTOM RIGHT *As the Allies moved from North Africa to Sicily, living conditions improved . . . well, that was a matter of perspective. This is the 27th Fighter Bomber Group's pilot ready room and parachute loft at Gela, Sicily. No doubt about it, this wasn't the States. Units like the 27th, with its A-36s, operated out of a continual series of forward airfields. Some were fortunate enough to be situated at abandoned villas in the lap of luxury, while others kept living in tents on bare scrub. No one said war was fair. Churchill had called the Mediterranean the soft underbelly of Europe, ripe for Allied conquest, rhetoric designed to get the Americans comfortable with his insistence on their participation. The soft underbelly turned out to be rock hard.* J. P. CROWDER VIA DOROTHY HELEN CROWDER

When the Fifteenth Air Force began flying strategic bombing missions into Germany from Italy, it quickly established itself as a significant strike force with B-24s, B-17s, P-38s, and P-51s. The AAF was finally able to pummel the Third Reich from west and south in the daytime while the RAF hit at night. Round-the-clock bombing had become a reality. These 759th Squadron, 459th Bomb Group Liberators from Giulia, Cerignola, have passed the IP (initial point) . . . bomb doors are open, seconds before bombs away. The blur is chaff, radar-reflecting foil strips that blanked German radar, preventing both effective tracking and accurate radar directed flak. JAMES WILSON

C-47s moved just about everything the military services needed in every theater throughout World War II. This 62nd Troop Carrier Group C-47 sits at Malignano Airfield,

Sienna, Italy, ready to onload a jeep and equipment for transport to the battle zone. Weather didn't mean much to transport pilots—you usually had to go no matter what. The proce-

dure in the flight manual for thunderstorm weather was "reduce power and enter." Vital matériel had to be there, regardless. ROBERT E. FRIZELL VIA KENNETH I. KAILEY

Capt. Charles "Gil" Gilbert with the 346th Fighter Squadron mascot, "Checkers," at Pisa, Italy. The 350th Group's P-47s were on the pointed end of the Twelfth Air Force effort to strangle enemy lines of communication up and down Italy. Though designed as a high-altitude interceptor, the Thunderbolt was a perfect ground-attack aircraft. EDWARD KREGLOH

A standard morning for the men of the 320th Bomb Group at Decimomannu, Sardinia, mid-1944. It didn't matter what a unit was flying—in this case B-26 Marauders—the army didn't discriminate on whether a base was blank or came with comfort. From one place to the next, conditions could change drastically, and bomb groups with more personnel didn't seem to have any more influence than a fighter outfit on airfield accommodations.

JOSEPH S. KINGSBURY

Drop-tank crate mansion at 14th Fighter Group HQ staff quarters, Triolo, Italy, complete with drop tank for the stove fuel. Every scrap of wood coming onto a base was worth using, particularly for housing, but heat remained a precious commodity, particularly here in the winter of 1944–45. The standard solution was 100-octane aviation fuel overhead in something like this discarded P-38 drop tank . . . it was dripped into a makeshift stove and lit. Problem was, it often blew the shack sky high. Hard to believe, but very few people were killed, and it remained a standard fixture. JAMES STITT

This 8th Troop Carrier Squadron C-47 is on a "blood run" at Naples: taking on whole blood for use on the front lines and in the field hospitals. Flight nurses and women in the blood-bank crews were continually in and out of range of enemy fire, and their skill had a significant impact on getting the job done. Few airplanes were better suited than the Gooney Bird for landing and taking off at the short forward airstrips at the front lines . . . just about anything one could cram inside, it could carry, unless an engine quit. Risk was an SOP (standard operating procedure).

ROBERT E. FRIZELL VIA KENNETH I. KAILEY

RIGHT *Although they were less flashy than the bomber and fighter boys, transport crews found their jobs more than rewarding at times. Here wounded are being unloaded at Naples from an 8th Troop Carrier Squadron C-47 under the supervision of flight surgeon Bob Frizell. This was heartbreaking work, absolutely vital to the war effort. Women in the combat zone? It's been done.* ROBERT E. FRIZELL VIA KENNETH I. KAILEY

A brand new, fresh-out-of-the-crate Allison engine being readied for installation on a 37th Squadron, 14th Fighter Group P-38 at Triolo by Technical Sergeant Jones (Engineering), Staff Sergeant Fred Colton (crew chief), and Sergeant Lenert (Engineering). There were no hangars to speak of for the units based in Italy, so ground crews worked on the airplanes outdoors, from fighters to bombers. Winter took no notice of this; bloody and frostbitten hands were not unusual, particularly as most mechanics could not work with the intricacies of modern aircraft wearing gloves. Throughout the entire Mediterranean campaign, the Germans held their positions with tenacity and at great expense to the Allies, draining resources and manpower at an alarming rate. What soft underbelly? JAMES STITT

FESTUNG EUROPA

The European Theater

Glider pilots were also infantrymen . . . who would spot any of these pilots as, well, pilots near their foxholes? This is 26 March 1945, the day after Operation Varsity, the aerial invasion of Germany. Once the glider had plowed into the earth and come to a stop, the pilots shouldered their rifles, put on their tin pots, and went off to war. In some operations the odds of survival were so low for the pilots and infantry aboard that planners hoped for nothing more than an initial taking of the objective. According to 98th Squadron pilot John Lowden, "Before a nighttime resupply of anti-tank artillery to Normandy, it was anticipated that 50 percent of the men and equipment would not be able bodied or usable after the landings."

JOHN L. LOWDEN

DICK PERLEY
P-47 pilot, 50th Fighter Group

One of the amazing things was the deluge of whiskey, brandy, wine, and champagne that landed on us during the winter of 1944–45, this in addition to the good scotch whiskey ration of, as I remember, two ounces for each mission, which the flight surgeon carefully doled out to each of us in our own bottle. We did some good jobs for Patton, so he sent a truck load of champagne to us—Piper Heitseig Cordon Bleu and Cordon Rouge. That is *good* stuff (all wedding and party champagne I have had since has been pretty bad). We had so much, we even staged "battles": champagne cork popping at each other between flights—like "A" Flight versus "B" Flight in our "Officer's Club"—a mess tent with some wooden walls with painted P-47s flying formation. It's a wonder we all didn't turn into alcoholics.

LEFTY GROVE
P-51 pilot, 4th Fighter Group

New and last P-51 assigned to me to finish my tour—Nov.–Dec. 1944. The dates are very hazy and conflicting, but the event is real and remembered. I had always filed in my mind that it was Van Chandler who had borrowed my aircraft and was killed in action, which resulted in my getting a new P-51D replacement. (My last assigned aircraft.) As time and years passed, the name of Don Emerson surfaced as the possible borrower and not Chandler. Yet log book recorded no notation concerning what pilot went down in my VF-T. My log book does reveal I flew a lot of other lettered aircraft, both in November and December 1944. Research reveals it was neither of these pilots. My log book *does* state that on December 6, 1944, I had an air test in new "tee," a P-51D-P-510-15.

I had heard somehow that a new P-51 was to be delivered from the States and that the group exec was earmarked for it. Well, that wasn't good enough for me, because I was not finished with my tour of combat. I was a regular pilot, and the group exec had no need for an assigned aircraft, since he wasn't flying regular missions. (At least I decided this.) So I got my dander up and went to see the new group CO, Col. Claiborne Kinnard. I made my point—I had no aircraft, needed an aircraft, a new aircraft was due in, and the group exec didn't need it, but I sure did. Col. Kinnard listened to me, and dismissed me, telling me to go back to the squadron. Squadron ops (in the same building) came out and told me the new aircraft coming in would be assigned to me. I was elated, but still sad that I lost my "old bird," and my wing-tip whistles.

The aircraft finally arrived and was immediately pulled into maintenance for the routine acceptance check. I had no idea who the pilot had been. When maintenance was complete and letters VF-T painted on it with the rudder painted the 336th Squadron color blue, C/C Johnny Ferra taxied it to the hard stand parking spot, which happened to be right in front of squadron ops. Johnny had it all open, cowling off, canopy open, just sitting in the breeze. As I came out of ops, I walked around it and chatted with Johnny as to the condition of the aircraft and its forms, then climbed up over the front left wing and got into the cockpit. *Wow!!* It hit me. The cockpit was as though someone had poured a gallon of sexy perfume all inside. It was now clear that a WASP [Women Airforce Service Pilot] was the previous pilot. I'm sure glad I hadn't been present when the new bird landed—it would have been difficult to concentrate on combat with such a fragrance in your nostrils. In combat when we weren't getting shot at, all I could think of was being home and makin' love. Some twenty-six to twenty-seven hours later all fragrance disappeared. Thank God for small favors.

ED CURRY
B-17 bombardier, 401st
Bomb Group

Combat was nothing like what we had done in the States in training, attacking through clear blue skies with no enemy interference. At the target we had people shooting at us, rockets coming at us, planes coming at us. And people hollering. It wasn't like in the movies, I'll tell you. They really screamed. We had one kid, a gunner, with a high, shrill voice. I can still remember him shouting excitedly over the interphone, "Pick him up, Paul, pick him up, Paul . . . Paul get 'im, get 'im, get 'im Paul!" Then other gunners would join in. You wanted to keep discipline over the interphone, but once the battle got going it was almost impossible.

We stole regular GI helmets, took them down to the base blacksmith's shop, flipped the guy a five-pound note, and he would hammer out the sides so that it would fit over our headgear. Also had my own special flak suit. I managed to get a spare section—other guys rounded up manhole covers—which I placed under my rear end, to protect the family jewels.

STAN WYGLENDOWSKI
armament officer, 406th
Fighter Group

V-1 attacks began on the night of the fifteenth of June 1944, and our landing strip (ALG-417) near Ashford, England, was right in line with Germany's launching sites for these V-1s, and London. We witnessed about 80 percent of those "Doodle Bugs" heading for London, and watched large numbers of them destroyed in the air, while others were shot down and exploded upon crashing into the ground. Some of them landed rather close to our air strip.

That first night these buzz bombs made their appearance, no one among us knew exactly what they were. Thus, in no time at all, rumors of all sorts began floating around as to the size of their warheads, how they were controlled, etc. There were even rumors of German paratroopers landing in the vicinity of our landing strip. Thus, our entire group was placed on alert, and the ground personnel in particular were dispersed throughout our occupied area. Roy Saux, one of our squadron pilots, anxious to help, says that he asked C. B. Kelly, our squadron CO, what he might do to assist. Kelly supposedly suggested that he gather up some of the flying officers in our unit, and guard against any possible invaders. Roy told me that he went back to his tent and rigged up a line of mess kits and other metallic gear on a string, strung them up around his tent, and went to bed, feeling certain that if any invaders showed up, the clanging of those metal utensils on the string would wake him up in time to repel or even capture some of these invaders.

When the other pilots came back from breakfast the following morning, they found Roy Saux fast asleep in his sack. He never heard the explosions of those buzz bombs that were being shot down and exploding in the vicinity of our air strip, let alone the rattling of his mess gear.

BERNIE LAY, JR.
B-17 co-pilot, 100th Bomb Group

A shining silver rectangle of metal sailed past over our right wing. I recognized it as a main-exit door. Seconds later, a black lump came hurtling through the formation, barely missing several propellers. It was a man, clasping his knees to his head, revolving like a diver in a triple somersault, shooting by us so close that I saw a piece of paper blow out of his leather jacket. He was evidently making a delayed jump, for I didn't see his parachute open.

A B-17 turned gradually out of the formation to the right, maintaining altitude. In a split second it completely vanished in a brilliant explosion, from which the only remains were four balls of fire, the fuel tanks, which were quickly consumed as they fell earthward.

EMIL DEMUTH
Fw 190 pilot, I./JG 1

I made my second attack on a B-17 on the left side of the formation, and one of my Schwarm members saw it go down. Then my wingman pulled away in an Abschwung and went down. This man's bravery had been in question, and Oesau had asked me to keep an eye on him. I dived away after him, to the south, calling him on the radio to join up with me. We did join up, and I led him in a climb back towards the bombers. Oesau had said that this man, an officer, had to get a victory. Coming back up from about three thousand meters, we came upon a single B-17 about two thousand meters higher, flying westwards away from the formation. The B-17 flew across our noses. (We were flying NE.) I resolved to lead the other pilot around and put him in a position where he could get his kill, from behind the bomber. Suddenly, my Fw shuddered under the impact of hits, and my cabin started to fill with smoke. Oil sprayed all over my windscreen. I pulled around sharply to the left and then, for the first time, I saw about five Thunderbolts coming down after me. Shortly afterwards my Fw was hit again, and this time it burst into flames. I jettisoned my hood and undid my straps. The flames were coming, and I was not protected by my oxygen mask or flying helmet. My wrists were burnt, as was my forehead, because the flames soon burnt through the thin parts of my cloth flying helmet. I had splinter wounds to my right hand and upper left arm. My watch stopped at 12.10, so I knew exactly when I had been shot down.

I kicked the stick away to the left, and I was thrown clear of the blazing aircraft. After a long fall, I pulled my ripcord, and my parachute opened. I saw that my trousers were on fire, and I hastily beat out the flames with my hands. I did not have any pain at this time—that would come later. I made a normal landing, rolled over on the ground, and released my parachute, which came away cleanly. First on the scene were three girls with bicycles. The first thing I asked them to do was to get the pocket mirror out of my jacket; I wanted to see the extent of the burns to my face. Those parts which had not been protected were lobster red. I was put on the luggage rack of one of the bicycles, and two of the girls pushed me along the road until we came to some German infantrymen out on an exercise. The soldiers pointed their guns at me, and I shouted at them: "Du Idiot! Weis nicht dass ich Deutscher bin?" [You idiot! Don't you know that I'm a German?] My wounds were bound up by one of the soldiers, and I was taken to the hospital at Minden, the nearest town.

HOWARD PARK
P-47 pilot, 406th Fighter Group

Although the Intelligence Report for August ends with a notation regarding 28th August, I flew a four-hour mission on the 31st of August. During this mission, our squadron came under flak fire while we were at low altitude. We couldn't spot the guns at first, but then I saw one gun site. I volunteered over the radio to "fly down his gun barrel" and proceeded to do just that. Unfortunately, we had head-on shots at each other, and an explosive shell hit the upper surface of my wing root on my right wing, glancing upward and exploding outside the cockpit. The wing and cockpit skin took the brunt, but one small fragment entered my face just under the right eye. No doubt from the stress, some small artery spurted a stream of blood about six inches from my face and soaked part of my pants and the parachute pack. I had no idea of the extent of my hurt, but I saw a lot of blood. On the return home the wound seemed inconsequential, but was tended by the group flight surgeon, who recommended the Purple Heart. I thought nothing of the incident until shortly after returning to civilian life, when my right eye began to fail. Despite extensive eye surgery in the Portland, Oregon, Veteran's Hospital, which had a top-notch eye surgeon, I completely lost the vision in my right eye.

DICK PARKER
P-47 pilot, 405th Fighter Group

We moved on to Glasgow for the new Thunderbolts. I never saw so many beautiful birds in my life. It seemed like hundreds of them all together ready to go. While getting assigned a new P-47, I strolled over to a closed hangar and saw a P-80 jet. I didn't know we had any in the U.K., but I guess we only used it for testing. I never did see any of them again. I finally found my P-47 parked behind some others in a rather tight formation. After checking it over, I thought I could taxi out without hitting anything. No one else was around to help me, so I started it up and it ran good. I locked the right brake, gunned it a little, but forgot the turning point was out on the right wing, and, in turning, I bent the left wing tip on the P-47 I was trying to miss. Of course, I was mortified to bring home a damaged plane. I stopped the motor to check the damage. Just the tip was ripped, but it didn't look like a flak hole. Still, no one came around, so I took out my Swiss army pocket knife, unscrewed the screws holding my left wing tip on, and replaced it with the left wing tip on the plane I hit. Shortly, I was airborne for St. Dizier with a perfect P-47—no damage. I'll bet they're still trying to figure out how that other P-47 had two damaged wing tips.

BERT STILES
B-17 co-pilot, 91st Bomb Group

I was there when the ship came in. One flak shell had burst just outside the waist window. The waist gunner wore a flak suit and a flak helmet, but they didn't help much. One chunk hit low on his forehead and clipped the top of his head off. Part of his brains sprayed around as far forward as the door into the radio room. The rest of them spilled out when the body crumpled up. The flak suit protected his heart and lungs all right, but both legs were blown off, and hung with his body, because the flying suit was tucked into electric shoes. Nobody else on the plane was hurt. The waist looked like a jagged screen. The Fort got home okay.

I climbed in with the medic, and, getting through the door, I put my hand in a gob of blood and brains that had splattered back that way. I took one look at the body and climbed out again, careful this time where I put my hands.

I felt no nausea, just a sense of shock, just a kind of deadness inside. I walked out beside runway 25 and sat down in the grass, and watched the high squadron peel off and come in. Then I remembered the blood on my hands and wiped it off on the grass.

One man gone, a million more to go, maybe even a billion before this is over. Maybe everyone in the world will get it this time. There are shells enough to go around. If some efficiency expert could just figure out a way, there would never have to be another war. We could wipe out the human race this time. The senselessness of it, and the ugliness of it, drove away all other thought for a time. Then the despair went away, leaving only doubt and a deep sadness.

MILT SANDERS
P-47 pilot, 406th Fighter Group

In southern England in April of 1944 the daylight stayed with us for a long time, and as the evening arrived, a small group would gather around Byron. He would bring out his record player and put on classical records. He would then sing in a most glorious bass voice with the music as his background, which could send shivers up and down your back. Then, too, there were times when someone would make a small fire so we could just sit around and listen. I didn't know Byron very well, but through his music, he made close friends of all those who heard him sing.

Sometime in August of 1944 on the return from a mission, he was missing, and no one noticed his absence until debriefing when he didn't show up. A number of times people got separated and came home late, but it didn't happen this time.

A month or so later, when we were on the continent, I was on a NAFFI trip from our base on a supply truck, and we stopped in traffic. I noticed a cross by the side of the road. Out of curiosity, I got out of the truck to see who it was. The name on the dog tags hanging on the cross was Byron L. Cramer. The world is missing the artistry of this man who was barely into his life.

FRED WEINER
POW, Stalag Luft VI

Sometimes the guards would steal from our Red Cross packages during inspections. We had to wait outside while they went through our stuff. So we'd wait until a can of instant powdered coffee was almost finished, then we'd fill it up again with stuff and spike it with cascara pills. Cascara, in those days, was a laxative. We used to shave it down and grind it up. It was a brown color and would blend with the instant coffee. You'd always know who stole the coffee, because he'd be on sick call the next day and he couldn't get back at us.

BELOW *The 56th Fighter Group lines up on the runway at Boxted for a mission, mid-1944. An excellent high-altitude fighter, the Thunderbolt could turn and roll with the best of them in protecting the bombers. When pilots were turned loose to strafe enemy installations and airdromes, the fighter proved so rugged and so effective, it quickly found a new mission, ground attack, in which it excelled as well.* MARK BROWN/USAFA

MIDDLE RIGHT *The last versions of the B-17G were modified for Cheyenne modification center tail turrets with better visibility and improved gun tracking. This 615th Squadron, 401st Bomb Group Fort is also a pathfinder—there is a radar hung from the ball turret position. Pathfinders led bomber formations, even when the target was obscured by cloud, to find targets by radar. The* lead radar bombardier would then call for all in the formation to drop on his signal. The results were not as good as expected, but it did keep up the pressure on a collapsing Third Reich. Pilot Alva Chapman put this airplane down at Melsbroek Airfield, Belgium, with two engines feathered on 11 December 1944 . . . it was later destroyed by strafing German fighters.* ROBERT ASTRELLA

TOP *Gear-retraction test on a 335th Fighter Squadron Mustang at Debden. Whenever the weather was half-decent, ground crews pulled as much maintenance as possible before it either rained or snowed again. Though the hangar facilities at Debden, an RAF base, were among the finest in the ETO, there wasn't enough room to do anything but major maintenance in the hangars.*
FRANCIS M. GROVE

BOTTOM *Republic's P-47 Thunderbolt was the Eighth Air Force's first fighter able to bash in the door to the Third Reich and punch German fighters in the nose. Rugged, with eight .50-caliber machine guns and the magnificent Pratt & Whitney R-2800 2,000-hp engine, the '47 was one of the largest single-engine fighters built, at a basic weight of seven tons. Yet it was surprisingly light on the controls, easy to fly, and able to outroll even the nimble Spitfire. The 56th Fighter Group introduced the aircraft to the theater and then elected to keep it to the end of the war instead of transitioning to Mustangs. This 56th P-47 is being gassed up at Boxted, England, fall 1944.* MARK BROWN/USAFA

Going on leave in London was magic, at least when the weather was good and no air raids were in progress. So much came out of the storybooks for Americans, who had heard of London Bridge, Westminster Abbey, and this vision of the tower of Big Ben, Parliament, and double-decker buses. In spite of the chaos of a city still under aerial siege, theaters and stores stayed defiantly open. Pubs were warm gathering places for lonely servicemen, and the Red Cross ran several establishments for GIs only.

MARK BROWN/USAFA

TOP *Although the P-38 Lightning made an overall poor showing in the Eighth Air Force due to a number of maddening technical glitches, it did quite well in the Ninth Air Force as a tactical fighter. With its four .50-caliber machine guns and single 20-mm cannon pointing straight ahead out of the nose, it was easy to aim and keep on target, whether strafing or in air-to-air combat . . . as Lightning pilot Erv Ethell said, "It was like spraying a garden hose." This 474th Fighter Group Lightning sits on a forward airstrip in Belgium, 1945.* JOHN QUINCY VIA STANLEY J. WYGLENDOWSKI

LEFT *In January 1945, the 7th Photo Group began to receive P-51 Mustangs to provide fighter escort for its unarmed F-5 Lightnings over enemy territory. This P-51D at Mt. Farm carries the simple group markings of blue spinner and red cowl stripe, plus the red rudder normally painted on 13th Photo Squadron F-5s. Working alone, armed with nothing but cameras deep in enemy territory, was a dangerous job. Out of the 7th's 4,251 sorties, the group reported 58 aircraft missing in action, among them 5 P-51s. Although the Mustangs recorded only a single probable and 1 damaged against enemy aircraft, they flew 880 sorties and no doubt kept the Germans away from their "Photo Joe" brothers.* ROBERT ASTRELLA

BOTTOM LEFT *England was a wonderland for Americans, who found the British people friendly, generous, and willing to act as family to lonely GIs away from home. Although they were somewhat separated by a common language, this was more fun than irritation, providing a mutual ground with the locals nonexistent in other theaters of war. This butcher shop in Luton was a beacon to hungry Yanks, who quickly found out the owners were having a rough time stocking anything due to the severe rationing of the day. Nevertheless, there always seemed to be something Mr. Dennis could squeeze out from the back. He quickly made loyal and fast friends.* ALEXANDER C. SLOAN

RIGHT *Supply section Sgt. Melvin E. Crooks shaving, Ninth Air Force style, at the 514th Fighter Squadron's first forward field on the continent after D-day. Tour-en-Bessim (coded A-13 on the planning map), France, was ahead of the Normandy beachhead at the base of the Cherbourg peninsula as the 406th Group and other 9 AF units kept up with the First and Third Armies in July 1944. You were lucky if the water was hot, but it didn't stay that way for long in the tin-pot helmet, which quickly became bathtub, kitchen, and soup bowl all in one.* JOHN QUINCY VIA STANLEY J. WYGLENDOWSKI

ABOVE *"Lefty" Grove's 4th Fighter Group P-51D gets a going over from crew chief Johnny Ferra and the ground crew at Debden, winter 1944–45. Fighting the war from England may have been more pleasant in some ways, but no one ever told the ground crews that in the winter, unless they wanted some dirty looks. The cold was bitter and damp* in Britain, penetrating to the very bones . . . sometimes it seemed you couldn't get warm, even standing next to a roaring pot-bellied stove in one of the Nissen huts. Grove held Ferra and his men in the highest respect, certainly higher than many officers who didn't appreciate the sacrifice ground crews made.* FRANCIS M. GROVE

BOTTOM RIGHT *The unheralded pilots of the war had the letter G, for Glider Pilot, in their set of army silver wings. Almost 6,000 American glider pilots were trained to fly 13,900 Waco CG-4A gliders . . . actually closer to flying bricks . . . and about 3,600 of those aircraft went into combat. The 98th Squadron, 440th Troop Carrier Group, is ready on a field in England—C-47 tow planes are lined up on the right, hooked to their CG-4As on the left by tow lines, each ready to take off in turn. Casualty rates ranged from 60 percent in Sicily to 25 percent in the Rhine River crossing. The odds on survival, or at least of coming away uninjured, were quite low.* JOHN L. LOWDEN

LEFT *Al Keeler in front of "GI Issue: Government Property," a B-17G Flying Fortress
with the 95th Bomb Group at Horam. His
leather A-2 jacket was the hallmark of army
pilots, an indivisible part of the pilot mys-
tique. It usually carried a name tag, leather
squadron patch, mission symbols, and some
form of art, probably a duplication of the
aircraft nose art, on the back. The other,
more famous army-pilot trademark Keeler
wears is the fifty-mission crush cap, something other services found disorderly and out
of character for military discipline. The idea
started innocently enough—take the stiffen-
ing band out so the hat can be worn with
earphones in flight, otherwise it wouldn't fit.
Soon the hat became rumpled and crushed,
particularly after fifty missions, thus the
term. It didn't take long for pilots who hadn't
even flown a mission to rip the stiffeners out,
roll the hats up, douse them in water and
trap them in a partially opened drawer or
under the mattress to get the effect . . . or
generally jump on them. Anything to bring
that aura of a hot-rock pilot.* ALBERT J. KEELER

A 490th Bomb Group Fort pulls out onto the runway at Eye just prior to takeoff for Germany, 1945. While other bomb groups became known as "hard-luck" units with high losses, the 490th seemed to have a guardian angel. Flying 5,060 sorties in 158 missions from the end of May 1944 to the last of April 1945, the group lost only 22 aircraft in action, the lowest losses of any Eighth Air Force bomb group during an extended period in combat. No one was complaining. ARNOLD N. DELMONICO

Phil Savides and Dick Perley look over a set of maps in an apple orchard for an upcoming mission just after flying their 50th Fighter Group P-47s from England to this forward operating strip inland from the Normandy beachhead, June 1944. The *group was to follow the troops all the way into Germany, basing at a series of rough, mud-laden airstrips just inside the front lines. The flying was demanding and more than a little dangerous.* RICHARD H. PERLEY

The results of 406th Fighter Group close air support . . . a burned-out German PzKw.V Panther tank. When Ninth Air Force P-47s went after targets, they pressed home until they were sure the job was done, under close liaison with the ground commanders. Pilots had a difficult time killing tanks because the Thunderbolt's .50-caliber guns would not penetrate the armor. One alternative was to ricochet the rounds just off the ground, hopefully a road or other hard surface, into the softer belly of the tank. Things changed significantly when large five-inch HVAR rockets arrived—one hit could knock out a tank. Howard Park of the 513th Squadron was the first pilot to kill a Tiger tank with one of the massive rockets. STANLEY J. WYGLENDOWSKI

TOP *A formation of B-17s from the 490th Bomb Group heads out from England for targets in Germany, pulling contrails. During the final year of the war, the Eighth Air Force became the largest aerial striking force the world had ever seen . . . or would ever see again. More than 2,000 bombers and fighters could be put up in a single day, stretching for well over 100 miles in an aluminum cloud, with 150,000 people in the aircraft or on the ground making it happen. According to historian Roger Freeman, "The daily logistical requirements could be enormous: some three million gallons of fuel, four thousand tons of bombs and four and a half million rounds of ammunition to give just the major items." In all, the Eighth did battle with Germany for 983 days.* ARNOLD N. DELMONICO

"Rusty" was the P-51K assigned to Jeff French in the 339th Fighter Group at Fowlmere. The only difference between the K and D model Mustangs was the propeller: the former had one from the Aeroproducts factory, while the latter had a Hamilton Standard with cuffs at the base of each blade. This winter of 1944–45 was not kind, with the ground covered most of the time by frost or snow. Before French finished his tour on April 5, 1945, "Rusty" was reassigned to Bill Preddy, brother of leading Mustang ace George Preddy. Tragically both brothers were killed in action: George by American gunners who mistook his P-51 for a German fighter on Christmas Day 1944, and Bill by enemy fire on 17 April 1945 near Prague. L. JEFFREY FRENCH

BOTTOM *Few realize that several Army Air Forces units flew British Spitfires carrying the American star-and-bar insignia. Among them was the 7th Photo Group, which flew camera-equipped Spitfire PR.XIs, like this 14th Squadron aircraft at Mt. Farm with fifty-two mission-completion marks on the side. The PRU (photo recon unit) Blue paint blended in quite well with the sky at high altitude. The deeper chin under the nose gave this version of the Spit somewhat less elegant lines than her fighter sisters, but there was no option in order to fit a larger oil tank for extended-range flying. Spitfires were known for short range, but the Mk.XI could fly to the deepest points in Germany with ease, high enough to make most German interceptors stall out trying to catch it. Unfortunately, the cockpit was cramped and noisy . . . better that than dead.* ROBERT ASTRELLA

TOP RIGHT *Three examples of Eighth Air Force fighter transition sit on this grassy stretch of England. "Hairless Joe" is the P-47D flown by David Schilling, commander of the 56th Fighter Group from August 1944 to January 1945, when the group decided to keep its Thunderbolts instead of transitioning to Mustangs. "Swede" is a P-51B flown by 339th Fighter Group pilot Duane Larson . . . this* model of the Mustang was the first to be committed to long-range escort over Europe, making the aircraft's reputation. "Arrow Head" is a new 339th Group P-51D with the improved all-round vision bubble canopy . . . though this slowed the airplane down a bit, the enhanced visibility in combat made this model the favorite of all the Mustang variants. ROBERT ASTRELLA

The pilot of "Shack Lassie" and wingman line up on the pierced-steel plank runway at the 364th Fighter Group's base, Honington, on 28 August 1944. The group had been flying Mustangs for a month after converting from the P-38. This pushed the pilots deeper into Germany . . . and into the action. During the last year of the war, the Luftwaffe was reluctant to engage fighters, going to bombers at all costs. In just over a year at war, the 364th lost 134 aircraft missing for 256.5 air and 193 ground kills claimed. The black-and-white D-Day invasion stripes were to show American anti-aircraft gunners the airplane was "friendly." Unfortunately, it didn't always work in the heat of combat, when anything moving got fired at. One gunner stated in his after-action report, "Fw 190s attacked us painted just like P-47s, but that didn't fool us and we got good hits." The planes were P-47s. MARK BROWN/USAFA

As Ninth Air Force fighter and bomber units moved up with the ground armies, staying just behind the front lines, AAF personnel got an up-close and personal look at the war. This infantry battalion jeep is stuck in the rubble and mud of what used to be a beautiful Cologne street, early 1945. Among those trying to wrestle it out is a German civilian. Such a contrast was becoming normal at this point in the war, as Americans saw the suffering they had brought on the German populace, which in turn came to depend on the new conquerors for basic sustenance. Just beyond this point, both sides were shelling each other across the Rhine River, each round whistling over the minor drama of a stuck jeep. STANLEY J. WYGLENDOWSKI

The Ninth Air Force strip at Asch, Belgium (Y-29), was a hub of activity in the last months of the war. A Thunderbolt of the 512th Squadron, 406th Fighter Group, taxies out for a mission loaded with bombs in early 1945, guided by the ground crew sitting on the wing tip as other fighters return. The P-47 was so blind on the ground that the pilot either had to S-turn to see around the massive nose or have a crewman look ahead for him. The dim conical slag pile from the local coal mine, on the horizon in the center, was always a dead give-away for the field. JOHN QUINCY VIA STANLEY J. WYGLENDOWSKI

The primary Eighth Air Force bomber was the Boeing B-17 Flying Fortress. These Forts from the 96th Bomb Group assemble for takeoff at Snetterton Heath in mid-1944. During the first five months of that year, the group sustained the highest loss rate of any Eighth Air Force unit. England may have been a wonderful theater of operations in which to live on the whole, but statistically the most dangerous place to fight World War II around the globe, whether on the ground or in the air, was in an Eighth Air Force bomber. The chances of completing a tour, twenty-five to thirty-five missions, was less than 25 percent, which meant someone passing his tenth mission should have been dead, statistically speaking. MARK BROWN/USAFA

TOP Forward airstrip, Belgium, 406th Fighter Group, 1944 . . . Howard M. Park's P-47D, "Big Ass Bird II," sits on the line with another 513th Squadron Thunderbolt ready for action. Both aircraft have bombs hung on the wing racks, and the upper gun-bay doors have yet to be fastened down. Flying out of the mud and muck of an unprepared strip, the 406th and other Ninth Air Force fighters kept the Germans down as Allied forces moved hedgerow by hedgerow toward Germany. During the Battle of the Bulge, the 406th was airborne almost constantly, including Park, who lost an eye in combat. STANLEY J. WYGLENDOWSKI

TOP *Reconnaissance came into its own during World War II, quickly developing from a help to an imperative capability. There were few more-effective recce aircraft than those based on the Lockheed P-38 Lightning airframe. It was a natural for quick modification to remove the guns from the spacious nose and replace them with cameras. Whether running at high altitude or on low-level "dicing" missions, Lightning pilots found few enemy aircraft could catch them until the advent of the Me 262 jet and Me 163 rocket fighters. This F-5E Lightning of the 13th Photo Reconnaissance Squadron, 7th Photo Group, is just starting its takeoff roll at Mt. Farm, England, early 1945.* ROBERT ASTRELLA

A 514th Squadron, 406th Fighter Group P-47D taxies along the perimeter track at Asch, Belgium, in early 1945. Crew chief R. C. "Pop" Everett took great pride in keeping the paint on his airplane . . . any weather or scrubbing of mud off the airframe usually took the decorative paint with it. With the primary job of maintaining airworthiness, ground crews viewed painting as a spare-time job, often done at night in the bitter cold of northern Europe. But it got done, much to the amazement of the pilots, who knew how hard the men were working just to stay up with the pace of combat. STANLEY J. WYGLENDOWSKI

TOP *Maj. Byron Trent, commander of the 333rd Bomb Squadron, 94th Bomb Group, wolfs down as much ice cream and sauce as he can manage—"I only ate two dishes"—at Bury St. Edmunds, 1945. England was better supplied than most theaters due to the fixed nature of its bases, particularly the RAF stations on loan to the AAF, but food was still a challenge. When something like ice cream was made, lines were long and shouts loud if it ran out before everyone got some.*

BYRON TRENT

Link Derick stands next to his 404th Squadron, 371st Fighter Group P-47D, showing the massive bulk of this rugged airplane. It was not unusual for Thunderbolts to belly in through forests, ditches, buildings, even stone walls, leaving the wings behind, with the pilot simply unstrapping and climbing out unhurt. Many jokes were made about the '47 by those who flew lighter airplanes, like the Mustang, but the joking stopped when someone saw a flying piece of junk bring its pilot home when anything else would have gone down.*

LINK DERICK

WOODEN DECKS, IRON MEN

The Naval Air Force

NORMAN STERRIE
TBD pilot, VT-2

We came aboard [the *Lexington,* which] was listing and smoking heavily but that was still underway and into the wind. My plane came to rest on an elevator, and as I stepped out of the plane I was lifted about two feet into the air as a major explosion took place below decks.

The ship was in bad shape, and we spent the rest of the afternoon on the aft deck, inhaling the smoke. We could not possibly have gotten off to the other carrier because our fuel supplies had been shut off. And I wasn't sure there would have been enough room to accommodate us on the other carrier without shoving their own planes over the side.

After taking in all that black smoke for several hours and being quite aware that we were ultimately going to have to leave the ship, we were quite relieved when the ''abandon ship'' order came. Many men slid down ropes into the sea. I dropped the life raft from a plane overboard and then watched it be swamped by survivors below, who pushed off without me. I went to another plane, got another life raft, and teamed with one of my buddies to hold it until I could get down, as well.

SCOTT MCCUSKEY
F4F pilot, VF-42

I looked up and saw three Japanese fighters heading toward us. I was flying wing on the right side of Leonard, who was watching our torpedo planes. I don't believe he saw the Japanese fighters. After the Japanese leader slowed down by fish-tailing his aircraft, he attacked. I pulled up over Bill Leonard to counter; now I'm their number one target.

The flight leader opened fire at about twelve hundred yards—pretty long range. He opened with his light 7.7s, then cut in his cannons. Initially, his bullets were coming straight at me, then fell astern. I was giving my attacker a full deflection shot in my endeavor to turn up into him and bring my guns to bear. His black and smoking tracer bullets seemed to be clawing at my tail. He dived under me, and I believe he became occupied with Leonard.

Now, the second Zero made his attack. I'd learned a bit from the first, and I timed my counteraction as I turned up into him, presenting an immediate full deflection shot. The Zero aborted its attack and made the mistake of pulling up in front of me: I put my pipper well ahead of him and he slowly pulled through my line of fire. He turned on his back and went straight into a dive, heading for the water. Smoke was observed coming from the leading edge of his wings, and it appeared that his guns were firing as he hit the water. The pilot may have been hit; his plane didn't burn.

Fueling-service crewmen and fire fighters wore red on flight decks, clearly evident here as a TBF Avenger is gassed up on deck. Technically, only fire fighters were allowed to wear red jerseys, while refueling crews wore a dungaree shirt and a red helmet. This was to avoid confusion in the event of a deck fire. It would appear this shot has been staged with fire fighters alone, most likely for the sake of a colorful scene.

I ducked into a cloud, since my speed was greatly reduced due to my zooming attack. When I came out of the cloud, there were two waiting for me, so back into the cloud I went. The cloud wasn't too big but sure was better than nothing—a fox hole in the sky. As I turned into the cloud, it was needle ball airspeed. Then, out I'd pop; then back in I'd go. The Zeros were waiting above the cloud for me. I needed altitude so I could attack, but the cloud I was running in and out of wasn't big enough. So I pushed the nose over to pick up speed, and with full throttle, I dived for the water and headed for the middle of the heavy weather ahead of the Japanese carriers.

As I headed home with my tail between my legs like an hound dog, I was disappointed in myself for running away from those Zeros. They had shocked the hell out of me. I didn't dream the Japanese had a fighter like the one I had fought against. Hell, those Zeros were going around me like a bunch of bees. I thought maybe the Japanese had captured some Spitfires or Hurricanes from the British.

MAX LESLIE
SBD pilot, VB-3

Although my 1,000-lb. bomb had dropped prematurely, I had to lead the squadron in the dive, as the initial dive made in a formation attack is the most important. When we got down to about 10,000 feet, I drew a bead on the target by firing my two .50 cal. fixed machine guns at the superstructure, which was on the starboard side one-third way aft from the bow. I did not receive AA fire. My bullets appeared to be hitting the bridge. When I got down to bomb release altitude, both guns suddenly jammed, and, in spite of my frantic efforts, they wouldn't recharge.

After leveling off from my attack, I look back just in time to see the second plane, piloted by Lt. (jg) Paul "Lefty" Holmberg, drop his bomb, which made a direct hit on the flight deck. It was the first bomb dropped in the battle. The bomb exploded in the midst of a pack of aircraft spotted just aft of the superstructure. The explosion turned the after part of the flight deck into sheets of flame and blew an airplane over the side just as it was being launched.

BOB DIXON
SBD pilot, VS-2

Scratch one flattop!

HENRY STRAUB
P-40 mechanic, 18th Fighter Group

One morning about daylight as I was turning up my aircraft, an F4F Wildcat was taking off from Guadalcanal's Fighter One. He was in trouble and hit the top of the trees. We could hear the crash, then smoke and flames soared above the jungle. After a while, a young marine pilot walked by with his parachute tucked under his arm. I asked him about the plane—he acknowledged it was his, but said as a result he would not miss the special breakfast of pancakes and eggs that morning.

MARION CARL
F4F pilot, VMF-221

On Guadalcanal, the situation as far as creature comforts—food and so on—were concerned was that they were pretty nonexistent at times. For instance, I think that for two weeks straight we ate nothing but Japanese food, captured food—canned fruit and canned meat—and it wasn't too bad. It didn't bother me. It bothered a lot of my squadron. Some of them were getting diarrhea and so on and so forth by not being too careful regarding the water they were drinking. But I don't remember ever being sick. I never got malaria, and some people figure I had a cast-iron stomach, but I'm just not a heavy eater, for one thing.

CHARLES A. LINDBERGH
F4U pilot, VMF-115

Other planes warm up as we taxi in. A new strike is getting underway. Leaf points of a coconut palm spear into the Southern Cross. A Marauder bomber drones off through distant night. The roaring fury of our war is replaced by damp, tropical silence. I smear bug repellent around my neck, and sit down on a grenade box. I can't wipe the vision of that church from my mind. Steeples don't fit into gun sights. Thoughts of God are antagonistic to the thoughts of war.

"I almost shot up a church today," I told a young Marine captain after we landed. "I just recognized what it was in time."

"Oh, you mean that little church on the Duke of York?" He laughed. "We strafe it on every mission. The Nips used to use it for their troops."

DAVID MCCAMPBELL
F6F pilot, VF-15

I got into an inverted spin inadvertently while making an overhead run on a Betty and was able to pull out with no strain and end up on the Jap's tail to shoot him down, which prompted my wingman to say, "What in the hell kind of a gunnery run is that!"

SABURO SAKAI
Zero pilot, Kokutai 265

Our pilots could not talk to each other, so we flew as individuals, where the Americans, especially the marines, flew as a team. I shot down over sixty aircraft, over forty were American. About thirty-four of those were American fighters. I fought the U.S. Army, Navy, and Marines. The army had faster aircraft, with P-51 and P-38 fighters. But the marines and the navy had the most durable. Once over the Philippine Sea, I fought an F6F Hellcat. I must have put two hundred rounds of my ammunition into it. I ran out of rounds and cannon shells. I could not believe the American was still flying. A Zero would have blown up after just twenty hits. The navy pilot saluted me as I pulled alongside, and I returned his salute, for he was a most valiant opponent. I instructed my pilots not to kill this man; he was true Samurai.

CHARLIE "HOT SHOT" HENDERSON
TBM pilot, VTN-90

Carefully, painstakingly, we eased up on our victim. One thousand yards and dead ahead, a black void with rain splattering on the canopy. He was cruising at about 140 knots and 4,000 feet, straight down Kamikaze Alley, the line of islands stretching from Kyushu to Okinawa.

One hundred yards, a black void. My fingers caressed the trigger. I could feel the sweat running down my back, yet it was very cold. Then a blur, darker than the dark, and the tail of a large aircraft appeared like a phantom, the exhaust from his starboard engine, maneuvering into position to fire. Then suddenly I saw the blur of his wings—an inverted V!

So intense was my frustration that I very nearly squeezed the trigger. How dare he not be Japanese! What was a Martin Mariner doing at this time of night in this place? Clearly he was friendly. Equally clearly, I was not. In truth, I had never in my life felt less friendly.

Finally I located his frequency on my data sheet. He was from that miserable PBM squadron operating near Okinawa. I called over the radio with a distinct Japanese accent: "All-same looksee starboard side, mellican boy." He pleasured me with a violent diving turn to port as he peeled off for the deck.

JACK COLEY
PBY pilot, VP-11

We were caught in several searchlights at once, and every ship in the anchorage was firing at us. It looked like a tremendous Fourth of July fireworks display with us in the center. I turned that PBY every way but inside out evading the gunfire. Long chains of tracers would come sweeping up, and it seemed that the gunner had taken the correct lead angle, but as I would turn and change altitude the tracers would miraculously curve and pass astern of us. With streams of tracers coming from all sides it was necessary to constantly change course and altitude.

A DOWNED AIRMAN

Thank God for the PBY.

DAVID MCCAMPBELL
F6F pilot, VF-15

Hellcat replacements came to us in late 1944 equipped with rocket rails. We in fighters had never been trained or even fired rockets before, but we took a quickie course with the torpedo bomber squadron and soon carried them or bombs on each flight. I used them on all occasions, but one day over the Philippines I spotted a Jap Francis, and after rather lengthy chase slipped onto his tail and let go with two of my air-to-ground rockets. One sheared off his tail fin without exploding, so after one of the crewmen bailed out, I moved in and let him have the .50-caliber treatment. Thus, I will never know whether the rockets were any good for air-to-air or not.

BOB DOSÉ
F4U pilot, VF-12

I had about two thousand hours in the air, an established fighter pilot in command of a squadron of real gung-ho guys. To the skipper fell the honor (obligation?) of choosing the most dangerous target for his division. I had long wondered quietly how I would react when the chips were down and unfriendly bullets were flying. I think most pilots do.

Our job that day was to suppress anti-aircraft fire so the bombers could attack with less opposition. I had selected the most threatening target for my division and rolled in smoothly from twelve thousand feet. The enemy opened up in return, and it was like flying into a hose jet of incandescent streaks. At about nine thousand feet, I opened up and remember thinking, How about that? Here I am, cool, calm, and collected. Great!

After the strafing run, I pulled out about one thousand feet and, still feeling cool and confident, opened up on another gun emplacement ahead of us. We then swept over the edge of the island and out to sea. I was feeling pretty proud, but my plane was shaking badly and I thought I'd copped a hit engine. But the gauges all looked OK. I glanced at the right wing and saw three guns firing. Then at the left wing. Three guns firing there, too. I looked at my right hand. My finger was wrapped tighter than hell around the trigger. I was (coolly and confidently) still firing my guns, spraying the horizon with bullets, and was sure the gun barrels were close to melting into pretzels. The others in my division, bless their hearts, never ratted on me.

BOB BUTCHER
F6F pilot, VBF-87

After lunch, Jim informed me there had been heavy kamikaze attacks and he had volunteered us for extra CAP duty. At 1500 we deck-launched—a more civilized method of departing the ship, I thought. When we were airborne, Jim radioed, "You're doing OK, Butch, so I'll take back Sugar and you fly wing on Bill." Sugar and I swapped places and Bill Hemphill repeated Jim's earlier admonition: "Just stay on my wing. If I want you to weave, I'll let you know."

We went to twenty-five thousand feet, then down to fifteen thousand, and finally to ten thousand, where we were vectored toward an incoming kamikaze—a Jill. When we spotted him and turned to intercept, Bill did a shrewd thing by sliding under Jim and Sugar to the inside of the turn. So, I slid under Bill, thinking, Hot damn! This'll put me on the inside and I'll get first crack at this baby. But about that time, Jim and Sugar and Bill began to fly around me on the outside of the turn, and I wondered what was the matter with the scow I was flying. My throttle was firewalled but I couldn't keep up. Then I sheepishly remembered I'd forgot to come out of high blower when we came down from altitude. As I pulled out of supercharger, Jim, Sugar, and Bill began to shoot. Seeing the shell casings pouring out of Bill's discharge chute, I thought, "Judas priest! I'll be killed by Bill's empties!"

The kamikaze shoot-down was better than any movie I'd seen. First, the left wheel fell out of the wheel well, then the plane began shedding parts and pieces. Just as I wondered if I'd make it through all the junk, the kamikaze exploded in a huge red fireball, throwing even more pieces in our way. Somehow we all made it through the junk. Who got the kill, I couldn't say, but I knew it wasn't me. I'd been so busy getting out of the way of falling shell casings and airplane parts, I didn't get my gunsight on the enemy.

The weather was lousy—lots of clouds—when fighter direction gave us another intercept vector.

"Go to formation X-ray," Jim radioed to Bill, and I wondered what the heck that meant. Apparently Bill didn't hear the call, so I keyed my mike and told Jim so.

As I broke out below, I saw the "bandit," a Judy, at my nine o'clock position. I called "tally ho," firewalled the throttle, and turned to chase him. I glanced back and the sight of the rest of the division breaking out below the clouds firmed my resolve.

The F6F was faster than the Judy, and the enemy pilot knew it. As a defensive move, he chopped his power. The next thing I knew I was not only catching him but was about to fly right by him. "Who said those guys are dumb?" I thought. I wasn't interested in finding out if a Judy could shoot, so I chopped power and dropped gear and flaps, too. I was over speed for that kind of stuff but, thank God and Grumman, the airplane held together. Even at that, I didn't get slowed down until I was flying wing—a real close wing—on the Judy. The enemy pilot and I stared at each other, eye to eye.

Just as I got my plane cleaned up, the Judy turned into me. I think he figured that if he couldn't get a carrier, he'd at least get me. His maneuver got one more notch of respect from me. I booted my F6F around, got on the Judy's tail and opened fire—short bursts at first. Then I held the trigger down and "walked" the tracers in. I was expecting the same kind of parts-flying-off spectacle seen earlier, but nothing like that seemed to happen. But I was getting hits, because the next thing I knew, the Judy flew into the ocean about the time I realized I was in immediate danger of following him in. His splash was as high as my wing tip as I flew past him into level flight.

The division rejoined and we returned to a ten-thousand-foot pattern for the rest of afternoon and evening, and things got *very* serious when it got dark. I'd never made a night carrier landing. I hadn't even been given the lecture, for Pete's sake! I radioed my concern to Jim Mantis, but he didn't seem too alarmed.

"It's a cinch," he said. "Just keep the top of the island on the horizon and you can't fly into the ocean."

It was *real* dark by the time we approached the ship, and I was nervous about Jim's island-horizon theory. I had to see *both,* and I wasn't sure I'd be able to see *either.* By the time we were in the landing pattern, nervous worked its way up to scared and I told myself, "You have one chance to get this thing on board. You'll never live to go around!"

Jim and Sugar got aboard on first pass. Bill got a waveoff. "Better him than me," I thought. My eyes latched onto the LSO's illuminated "skeleton" suit, and I prayed my rubber-band legs would hold out until I got aboard.

My landing was beautiful. At least nobody challenged it. More terror: I thought they were going to taxi me over the bow when they spotted me at the front edge of the starboard cat. Then, after deplaning, the voice on bullhorn blared, "Ensign Butcher, report to captain on the bridge."

"What now?" I thought, but I was so glad to be alive I really didn't care.

A navy 20-mm anti-aircraft gun crew sits it out on an airfield in the Aleutian Islands, which ran seventeen hundred miles off the end of Alaska . . . more like the end of the world. The Japanese invaded the Aleutians in June 1942 as a diversion for their attack on Midway and as a buffer against long-range U.S. bombing missions over the home islands. Thanks to the great Magic code-breaking success, American planners were not suckered in and the arctic war became a stalemate. Nevertheless, the islands were fortified with U.S. Army and Navy units and combat was constant, though the brittle weather was the main enemy for both sides. Japan finally called it quits and pulled out in August 1943. NATIONAL ARCHIVES VIA STAN PIET

The Consolidated PBY Catalina was a flying anachronism in World War II. In spite of first entering the fleet in October 1936, this slow and vulnerable patrol plane made its way through every combat zone to rack up an outstanding record. This PBY-5A, the first amphibious version with retractable landing gear, sits on the ramp at NAS Norfolk, Virginia, 1942. Though the modification weakened the hull and lowered the already impossibly low top speed, it gave the boat an unprecedented versatility. By the time the war ended, more Catalinas had been built than any single seaplane in history, even though faster and more sophisticated aircraft were available. NATIONAL ARCHIVES VIA STAN PIET

BELOW *Operation Torch, the Allied invasion of North Africa in November 1942, was the first chance the Americans were given to put troops in combat against the Germans. The navy supported the operations with flattops, including lighter escort carriers such as the* Sangamon, *here loaded with SBDs and F4Fs. The deck is chalked with bearings and distance to home base. The aircraft have had their national insignia painted with a yellow surround, a device dreamed up to identify American aircraft during the invasion.* NATIONAL ARCHIVES VIA STAN PIET

When the F4U-1 Corsair went into navy service in October 1942, it encountered some insurmountable problems during carrier trials, and the fighter was relegated to operating with navy and marine squadrons from land bases. The initial "birdcage" canopy and low pilot seat did not give near enough visibility over the long nose, particularly in the "groove" on final. The landing gear had so much spring the aircraft bounced too high when it hit the deck, often skipping over the arresting ca-bles. With the F4U-1A came a new bubble canopy, a higher pilot seat, and improved landing gear, making the Corsair an excellent carrier fighter. When the war ended, the F4U had some fourteen hundred enemy aircraft claimed destroyed to its credit, for a kill-to-loss ratio of eleven to one. Of all navy fighters, pilots considered the Corsair the best air-to-air machine—maneuverable, light on the controls, fast, with a superior roll rate. NASM ARNOLD COLLECTION

BOTTOM RIGHT *In the Aleutians, it was too cold to worry about command distinctions and interservice rivalry. This look at arctic summer on 19 July 1943 shows a mix of army and navy activity, with P-40Es and PBY-5As on the line. The indispensable Cletrac-treaded tug pulls one of the Warhawks across the line . . . this* thing could get just about anything stuck in anything out. Line chiefs and mechanics didn't have much protection from the weather, but tents were better than nothing, and nothing seemed to be standard in this near-forgotten theater of war. NATIONAL AR-CHIVES VIA STAN PIET

LEFT *A PBY Catalina patrols a stretch of the Aleutian Islands in March 1943. The VP communities often had more range in their Catalinas than they wanted. Doing just over 100 mph in cruise, it could fly close to 3,000 miles . . . a turn of the E6B "whiz wheel" puts that at something between 25 to 30 hours in the air, well beyond the endurance of even those airplanes with two sets of pilots. Yet it was not unusual to fly well into exhaustion under the pressures of war when sighting the enemy could mean the difference between victory or defeat. It was a PBY that reported the first sighting of the Japanese fleet approaching Midway.*
NATIONAL ARCHIVES VIA STAN PIET

RIGHT *With the coming of the Grumman F6F Hellcat, the U.S. Navy had a fighter that could beat the Zero, protect the fleet, and carry out air-to-ground strikes. When the Hellcat entered combat in August 1943, the entire complexion of the Pacific air war changed almost instantly. In just two years of action, navy Hellcat pilots shot down 4,947 of the 6,477 Japanese aircraft claimed destroyed in the air. Besides having excellent firepower and armor, the F6F was easy to fly, particularly when landing on a carrier . . . it remained controllable even in a full stall. Gene Valencia, a Hellcat ace with VF-9, didn't mince words about his feelings: "I love this airplane so much that if it could cook I'd marry it."* NASM VIA STAN PIET

TOP RIGHT *Through the 1920s and 1930s, the navy put a great deal of stock in scouting aircraft, which were catapulted from battleships and cruisers and then recovered at sea. With the advent of such excellent carrier-borne scouts as the SBD and the increased inventory of carriers, the need for scout floatplanes quickly disappeared. This Curtiss SC-1 Seahawk* was the last, and possibly the most aesthetically pleasing, of the scouts designed to serve on ships without flight decks. The first SC-1s were assigned to the USS Guam in October 1944, but there was little action for them before the war ended. This Seahawk is parked on Saipan, mid-1945. EDWARD W. SIMPSON, JR.

BOTTOM RIGHT *An aircraft carrier's flight deck ran on the courage, efficiency, and coordination of its deck crews. Certainly in one of the most dangerous jobs in the navy, not only were these men often in harm's way, but they could be blown overboard by high winds or prop blast, mangled by folding wings, and chopped apart by whirling propellers. Working in three* sections, the men were identified by colored jerseys and cloth helmets to avoid any more confusion than was already there. Virtually all aircraft moves were made by blue-shirted and -helmeted handling crews of twelve nonrated seamen, such as these lashing an SBD to the deck. NATIONAL ARCHIVES VIA STAN PIET

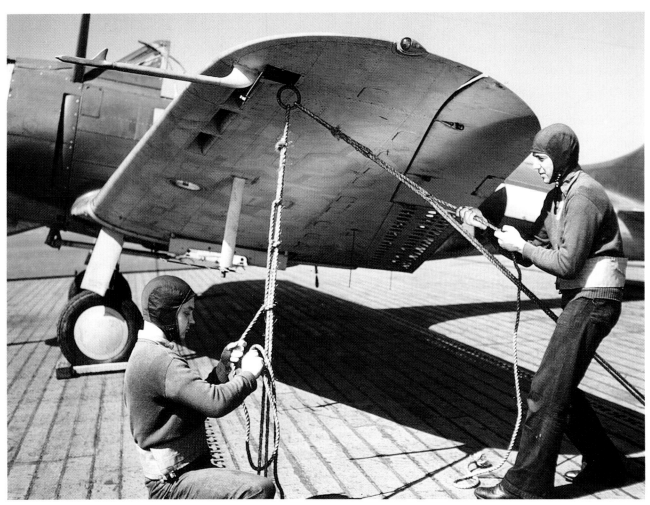

Air Group 9 aboard the recently commissioned USS Essex (CV-9), 20 March 1943. With the Essex came a new series of large carriers that would dominate the Pacific Ocean for the remainder of the war, each capable of operating eighty to one hundred aircraft. As a result, larger air groups with modern, deadly aircraft would clear the skies of Japanese aircraft and hit enemy ground installations constantly. On deck are new F6F-3 Hellcats of VF-9 and "slow but deadly" SBDs of VB-9, which would join in their first combat against Marcus Island on 1 September 1943. Though the Dauntless was supposedly obsolete, it continued to do an outstanding job throughout the war at the hands of well-trained pilots and experienced commanders. U.S. NAVY

BOTTOM RIGHT A yellow-jerseyed and -helmeted plane director has just handed off a Hellcat to a fellow taximan after the fighter has landed aboard the USS Lexington (CV-16), 1943. Nothing on a carrier moved unless these petty officers and chiefs made it happen. The color-coded system worked quite well, particularly in the confusion of combat, when a glance at a color immediately communicated what the man was asking for. With little variation, this system has continued through the years to the present day. NATIONAL ARCHIVES VIA STAN PIET

An F6F-3 from "Fighting Five" (VF-5) sits running in the chocks prior to launch from the newly commissioned USS Yorktown (CV-10) in May 1943. In August, VF-5 would become the first navy fighter squadron to launch the Hellcat into combat, over Marcus Island. The blue-jerseyed handling crewman has his hands on the chocks, ready for the signal to pull them away so the pilot can move up to the launch position, then make a running takeoff. U.S. NAVY

Lt. Cdr. David McCampbell in the cockpit of his F6F-5 Hellcat, "Minsi III," on 4 November 1944. He would go on to become the navy's leading ace, with thirty-four confirmed kills and the Medal of Honor. As commander of Air Group 15 aboard the Essex, *he shot down nine enemy aircraft, plus two probables, on 24 October 1944 during the Battle of Leyte Gulf, a single-mission score unsurpassed by any American pilot in history. During the same sortie, his wingman, Lt. Roy Rushing, knocked six aircraft down. By the time the war ended, Air Group 15 was credited with downing more aircraft and sinking more ship tonnage than any other unit in the navy.* NATIONAL ARCHIVES VIA STAN PIET

Hellcats of Air Group 5 aboard the Yorktown, *led by Lt. Cdr. Jimmy Flatley, Jr., prepare to launch for Marcus Island on 31 August 1943, the combat debut of the F6F. By this time the three-color camouflage paint has already suffered from operating at sea, with several overspray repairs and exhaust stains the rule rather* than the exception. *Rarely did anything remain pristine in salt air and under combat conditions—if the airplanes ran and came home, that was often enough. With large drop tanks, Hellcats had plenty of range to seek out the enemy with a variety of ordnance.* NATIONAL ARCHIVES VIA STAN PIET

New F6F-3s over Treasure Island and the Oakland Bay Bridge in early 1943 as the Hellcat was working its way into squadron service. With its big wing, the fighter was as close to the perfect carrier aircraft as any company came during World War II . . . and for some time after. It actually came aboard five miles per hour slower than its predecessor, the F4F Wildcat, which was something considering how much larger the F6F was. After about twelve field-carrier landing-practice (FCLP) hops, pilots were quite comfortable bringing it aboard ship for the first time. U.S. NAVY

Grumman Aircraft Company products dominated carrier decks for much of the war, evident here aboard the USS Cowpens *(CVL-25) during the Marshalls/Gilberts campaign in late 1943. These TBF Avengers of VT-25 and Hellcats of VF-25 are warming up for launch. The "Mighty Moo" was one of nine light carriers built on cruiser hulls. Though initially equipped with SBDs, the CVL air groups dropped their Dauntlesses in favor of more F6Fs, standardizing on the Hellcat-Avenger combination. The F6F became an excellent dive bomber and ground-attack aircraft, particularly in VBF units, carrying bombs and rockets to a variety of targets.* U.S. NAVY

A fighter pilot's view of the invasion of Tarawa in the Gilbert Islands, 22 November 1943. Ed Simpson looks down from his VF-35 F6F Hellcat at Betio Island, site of the main landing with its airstrip and pier, in sight below . . . landing craft are scattered just off shore. Simpson and his fellow Chenango pilots were covering the 2nd Marine Division pushing east up the middle of the island after two days of bloody fighting, some of the worst of the war up to that point. Four days after the marines hit the beach, Tarawa was taken, but it cost some 3,300 American casualties, including 1,027 dead. Of the 4,836 Japanese defenders, only 17 wounded survived. EDWARD W. SIMPSON, JR.

LEFT A brand new Curtiss SB2C Helldiver gets a load of ammunition before initial gunnery and bombing practice. ARNOLD/NASM

The Vought OS2U Kingfisher served the fleet throughout the war, flying from a number of ships equipped with catapults. ARNOLD/NASM

Yellow-jerseyed plane directors oversee respotting of the Lexington's *Hellcats to Fly III before a mission in 1945. A wartime carrier flight deck was controlled by dividing it into three sections. Fly I—launching and catapult area, directed by flight deck officer and catapult officer. Fly II—amidships, with the island, under the taxi signal officer. Fly III—aft, the landing area, with the landing signal officer and arresting gear officer. The deck crew, with their multicolored jerseys and helmets, reigned supreme in each of the three sections . . . their word was law, or some serious accidents would follow in short order.*
NATIONAL ARCHIVES VIA STAN PIET

BOTTOM RIGHT *Above the Pacific, 1945—the* Chenango's *air group outbound for a target. Avengers lead the pack, covered by Hellcats, including an F6F-5(N) night fighter with a radar fixed to the right wing. Though escort carriers were slow (at best eighteen or nineteen knots), they provided the extra striking power needed to bring large aerial attack forces to bear on important targets. When combined with light carriers (CVLs) and the larger CVs, the U.S. Navy dominated the globe in seaborne aviation. Like many smaller carriers, the* Chenango *was originally commissioned in 1939 as a different vessel, in this case the mercantile tanker* Esso New Orleans. *She was reclassified and modified by the navy, then recommissioned in June 1941.*
EDWARD W. SIMPSON, JR.

One of the war's early genuine heroes, Edward H. "Butch" O'Hare became the U.S. Navy's first ace, getting five kills against Japanese aircraft while flying F4F Wildcats with VF-3 off the USS Lexington *on 20 February 1942. Intercepting a formation of incoming Mitsubishi G4M (Allied code name Betty) bombers, he claimed five destroyed in four minutes. In April he went to the White House, where President Franklin D. Roosevelt gave him the Medal of Honor for the action. Later that year O'Hare returned to combat on the* Enterprise *to pioneer navy night-fighter operations in the F6F Hellcat. Tragically, on 26 November 1943 he was shot down and never recovered.*

The USS New Orleans *cruises ahead as an Avenger launches from the* Yorktown *during combat ops in 1944. After the Battle of Midway, the Grumman TBF, later built as the TBM by General Motors, became the navy's primary torpedo bomber. Although dropping torpedoes at close range against an enemy task group proved near suicidal, the Avenger racked up quite a record against Japanese merchant shipping in the Pacific and German U-Boats in the Atlantic. It was a big airplane, very heavy on the controls, which had to be pushed and shoved around to maneuver at all . . . but this also made it rock stable on bomb and torpedo runs.* NATIONAL ARCHIVES VIA STAN PIET

Grumman's stubby F4F Wildcat, "a beer barrel on a roller skate run through with an ironing board," was the navy's only major fighter during the first year of the war. Though outclassed in speed, maneuverability, and range by the Japanese A6M2 Zero, the Wildcat could absorb battle damage, had superior armor protection, could dive away from the Zero, and had excellent .50-caliber machine guns to chop up light enemy fighters and bombers with little problem. Through superior tacticians such as Jimmy Thach, who invented the mutual covering "Thach Weave," the F4F became a most formidable fighter, holding the fort in the darkest days of the Pacific War. NATIONAL ARCHIVES VIA STAN PIET

*A plane captain has just started "East
Orange," the F6F-3 Hellcat of VF-
35 pilot Ed Simpson attached to the
USS* Chenango *during its Pacific
War cruise of 1944–45. The name
was for Simpson's hometown in New
Jersey. The* Chenango *was among
the class of escort or "jeep" carriers
(CVEs) built for antisubmarine work,
convoy protection, and amphibious-* landing close-air support as well as a
host of other duties. During Opera-
tion Torch, the ship carried Army Air
Forces 33rd Fighter Group P-40s
into the area and launched them for
French Morocco. She then sailed for
the Pacific with a full complement of
aircraft, primarily F6Fs and TBMs,
to cover island invasions such as that
on Tarawa. EDWARD W. SIMPSON, JR.

PACIFIC SWEEP

The Pacific Theater

Two 19th Fighter Squadron ground crews sweat it out in the shade of their P-47 on Saipan, December 1944. Once the 318th Group was settled in, the war became a long, hot struggle against not only the enemy but also the elements, seen by the mud on the tires and the undersurface of the wing. By this point the unit's battered '47s were flying fourteen-hundred-mile round-trip escort missions to just south of Iwo Jima for Seventh Air Force B-24s, an excruciating experience for pilots sitting on rock-hard seat pack parachutes. They would do the job until longer-range P-38s, P-47Ns, and P-51Ds began to replace the weary aircraft. PAUL
THOMAS/BOB RICKARD

MANFORD SUSMAN
ground officer, 433rd Troop Carrier Group

In the beginning we'd tried to buy pigs from the [New Guinea highland] natives, but met a peculiar resistance to the idea. It seemed that their pigs were their most prized possessions and they had no intention of parting with them. Our interpreter explained that we needed meat, and they seemed to understand. Muttering that they'd be right back, the party of natives disappeared toward their village. Our mouths were watering at the thought of some nice fresh pork—and then they returned. With them were several girl children from the village. "Meat," said the headman happily. "Meat for you to eat." We radioed for more salt and some kind of eatable meat.

JOHN STEGE
P-38 squadron commander, 347th Fighter Group

Once I threatened to strafe a control tower returning from a particularly bad mission. I only did that because they ordered one of my P-38s, when he was trying to land on one engine, to go around and let a C-47 take off first. The pilot spun in on the end of the runway and was killed. I was so mad, I told them if they didn't let my pilots in trouble have priority, I'd strafe them the next time we didn't get a green light. After I landed, I went up into the control tower and told the 1st Lt. off in a few short words. I was grounded for thirty days, and I did get into trouble, as you can see from the citation. Hey, they were on our side and only doing a job. I was out of line, but all my pilots bought me several drinks after that.

APO 719
1 March 1945
Subject: Violation of Flying Regulations

To: Commanding Officer, 13th Air Service Center, APO 719

1. At approximately 1200, this date, a flight of P-38's were buzzing WAMA strip (East to West) prior to landing. The tower informed operations that he had flashed a red light to leader. A C-47 had previously been cleared for west to east take off. The flight of P-38's broke for landing and formed pattern disregarding tower's red light. Tower shot parachute flares when they were on final approach and they went around.

2. After they had landed, the flight leader sent an M.P. to base operations, asking to have the officer in charge come to see him. I went over to see what he wanted. He confronted me in a belligerent attitude and wanted to know "What the hell was wrong with the tower operator." I told him they informed

me that they had given him a red light when buzzing and he had evidently disregarded it.

3. He then informed me that his outfit was based here and it was their field and they were running things here. He also stated, "The next time I buzz the tower and receive a red light on account of a C-47, by God, I'll strafe the tower even if I have to stand courts martial for it." I then left him to return and get a full report from the tower operator. These planes were arriving unannounced from Clipper Tower, Dulag, Leyte. I later discovered that this pilot's name is Major John Stege, 68th Fighter Squadron, 347th Fighter Group.

4. A statement by T/Sgt. Charles R. Otto, tower operator, is inclosed herewith.

> Harry A. Duckworth,
> 2nd Lt., Air Corps,
> Ass't Operations Officer

JOHN TILLEY
P-38 pilot, 475th Fighter Group

During stateside training I had been told many times never to attempt to turn with a Jap fighter. Everyone agreed it was a good way to get creamed. I believed! Before going into combat I was told by all the "old hands" who bothered to talk to me "never turn with a Jap, it's suicide." I believed, I believed! The first time I got behind one of those made-in-Japan secret weapons called a Zero, I was looking at his tail one minute and the next thing I knew I was looking at the same guy coming at me head on. I still don't know how he got that thing cranked around so fast, but brother did I ever BELIEVE!

JOHN STONE
B-25 pilot, 345th Bomb Group

As my truck moved along, a Japanese white phosphorous bomb exploded, causing the entire jungle landscape to light up as if it were midday. The truck continued to move, but at the next opportunity, after more bombs had been dropped, the entire complement bailed out and ran off the road into the shelter of trees. I ran for some two or three hundred yards, hearing the explosions of bombs and trying to escape the holocaust if one came close to me or the trucks on the road. A short time later, a Japanese reconnaissance plane dropped another bomb and illuminated the area where I had hidden. I was in the middle of a bomb dump.

FRANK SHEARIN
P-38 pilot, 54th Fighter Squadron

We were on a mission to Attu, carrying a full load of ammunition, one 1,000-pound bomb and a 165-gallon external fuel tank. After about an hour on course, Lt. Michael Clemens aborted and returned home. We later found out that Mike had asked for and been given two pieces of Chicklets chewing gum, or so Mike had thought. The Chicklets had turned out to be Feenamint laxative. Michael Clemens never did ask anyone for chewing gum after that.

ANDY ANDERSON
P-38 pilot, 475th Fighter Group

We of Possum Squadron played chicken at Dobo by seeing who would slam on the brakes of his jeep to keep from crashing into the creek, which was near the entranceway to the meadow where the 475th was based. I can well recall riding on the hood of a jeep traveling at 40 or 45 mph and grabbing everything in sight when my driver decided that the other jeep wasn't going to stop and we were going to wind up in the ditch if we didn't stop ours.

HENRY STRAUB
P-40 crew chief, 18th Fighter Group

The sky was full of planes; there were dogfights all over the place. Then, two of our aircraft buzzed the field, so we ran back to the service area. It didn't matter which crew was responsible for a given P-40 during such action; everyone helped to refuel and reload the guns. The engine was quickly checked for hits and the oil level checked. Someone would give the pilot a drink of water, then we'd cheer him off again. "Go! Go! Good luck, Lieutenant!"

Just as those first two P-40s took off to return to the fight, someone shouted, "Look out! Zero!" I had seen this one approaching from the north over the trees, but I thought it was an F4F. The Zero made a strafing run on us, but there was indeed an F4F right on his tail. I ran like mad for the bunker, dived in head first, and landed on two friends from back home. Some reunion.

ANDY ANDERSON
P-38 pilot, 475th Fighter Group

Possum Squadron had a five-gallon milk can which was used for our binges. At Nadzab we began a day by pouring all the booze in the milk can. By mid-afternoon most of the flying officers of our squadron were gassed. An enlisted man who walked by squadron CO Warren Lewis's tent was dragged in and given a drink. He was then advised that the officers of the 433rd were challenging the men of the 433rd, the enlisted men that is, to a baseball game. In the moments that followed, every sergeant in Possum Squadron showed up. The milk can was placed at home plate and the only way you could get a drink out of it was to score a run by crossing home plate.

The enlisted men beat the officers by a score of something like twenty-eight to fifteen, and in the end everyone just sat down and drank the can dry. At one point in the game, group CO Col. MacDonald heard the screaming, swearing, and shouting, so he strolled by to see what was going on. He just shook his head after observing the situation for a few moments and walked away without saying a word. Just as well. Those crazy bastards probably would have shoved his head in the milk can and drowned him.

At still another point in the game, Lt. Al Pomplun was playing right field, and a long, high pop fly was hit in his direction. To the shouts of "Catch it you sonovabitch," he staggered about the field and finally put up his mit . . . I'll be damned if the ball didn't hit it dead center and the enlisted man was out. Al just stood there, weaving back and forth, looking down at his glove. Somehow we always managed to get a squadron in the air the next day, and we did the following day without any trouble at all.

VIC AGATHER
B-29 project officer

The engine fire problem centered around the overheating of the exhaust valves . . . the engine would swallow the valve and in most cases this resulted in an engine fire. If the engine fire could not be contained within the forward section and reached the accessory housing, the magnesium, which burns at extremely high temperature, would burn through the firewall into the main spar, and the wing would peel off with the loss of the airplane.

WAGNER DICK
B-29 pilot, 498th Bomb Group

Our radio was shot out. I didn't know it then, but our rudders were held on by only one strand. Without oxygen we were forced to drop to about nine thousand feet and lost Kuenning in the soup. The No. 4 engine picked up some power in the lower altitude, offsetting the drag of the windmilling No. 1. Then No. 3 started leaking oil. The No. 2 was hit by flak fragments but was undamaged. Sparks flew from the windmilling prop and the hub became so hot from friction that it glowed in the darkness. The left gunner said he thought it was the moon coming up when he saw the reflection of the white-hot glow. Halfway home the propeller flew into space. Shortly afterward the plane broke out of cloud, and the navigator made his first celestial fixes and announced in pleased tones, "We are halfway home already—we ought to make it after all."

C. J. GRAHAM
OA-10A pilot, USAAF detachment, 231 Group, RAF

Life rafts on B-29s weren't provided with enough flares, and the men in the rafts didn't know how to use what they had. Air crews especially needed training in signaling techniques and equipment. A man in a dinghy will fire a Very pistol square at you every time, rather than at ninety degrees as he should. By doing this, your attention is attracted to the trail of smoke. If he shoots it right at you, all you see is a tiny red dot.

From five hundred feet a dinghy looks like a spool of thread. There are so many reflections on the water that it's difficult to distinguish a raft from them. I've seen sharks and big turtles the same color as a raft; I've circled some for hours. Even after you see a dinghy on the water it's hard to hold it, unless it's a perfect day. When we'd find a raft I'd keep my eye on it while the copilot flew the plane.

I rescued thirteen men one time because one man out of the thirteen knew how to use the signal mirror with the little cross on it. That was the only thing that saved them.

I landed one night about one o'clock contrary to orders and was almost court martialed for doing it to pick up the crew of a B-29 snooper plane. It had come up from Singapore, run out of gas, and floated for four days. A B-24 was circling him, as well as two RAF Cats. They told me not to land on the water at night, but I did, and we pulled twelve living men and one dead one on board. We had a tough time getting off. The first try the ship yawed to the right; the wing tip float hit the water and I had to try again. After a run of about three miles, she picked up, then hit five times before we got off.

SAM HANFORD
B-29 pilot, 499th Bomb Group

Several thousand feet near Osaka we noticed the updraft and smoke were bad but didn't think anything of it until daybreak, when the co-pilot looked out and saw something the size of a desktop clinging to the leading edge of the wing. Back at Saipan we discovered it was a badly burned tin roof. It wasn't that we were flying low, it was just that that damned roof was flying so high.

LOUIS AVRAMI
B-29 navigator, 504th
Bomb Group

Just then the plane flipped over on her back and headed straight back toward the target, flying belly up. I looked down through the bomb bay to see the fires, and instead there were the stars and the moon. Then I looked straight up and saw the fires. For a minute I thought I was dead.

JIM GILL
P-61 pilot, 6th Night
Fighter Squadron

A radar observer bailed out one night over Iwo Jima. His night fighter was making an intercept on a bogey. A marine night fighter was up making an intercept on the same bogey, only he was actually intercepting the Black Widow. Of course, the radar observer on the Black Widow was concentrating on his interception, and, all of a sudden, here came a bunch of tracers at his tail cone. He didn't know what the heck was going on, but he didn't wait to find out, so he opened his hatch and bailed out safely into the water. He floated around in his raft all night long—got picked up the next day.

PRESTON GERMAIN
P-47 pilot, 318th Fighter
Group

Ie Shima was a difficult island to fly from because the runway had a hump in the center and went downhill towards both ends—north and south—and at either end had a very definite cliff. When we took off on long-range missions carrying two five-hundred-pound bombs and rockets plus the enormous quantity of fuel the P-47N carried, it was a question whether or not we could get off the runway. The pilots we lost were those who failed to get airborne even after jettisoning their rockets and bombs two-thirds of the way down the runway.

We later solved this problem by stationing a flying officer halfway down with a portable radio set so that he could tell pilots who weren't going to make it to jettison their rockets, bombs, or napalm tanks at an earlier point. Even then many of them would barely wobble into the air at 108 mph, sometimes dropping out of sight momentarily as they came off the end of the runway and went over the cliff.

BILL GOODRICH
B-25 pilot, 17th
Reconnaissance Squadron

I called back to the gunner to ask if he could see any damage, as the plane was extremely sloppy on her controls. He said, "Jesus Christ, Lieutenant, the whole right tail section and rudder is gone. The waist gun was blown right out through the side of the ship and we're full of holes. Are we going to ditch?" I told him, "Hell no, I can't swim that far."

As we neared home base at Lingayen, several planes came up to look us over as the flight which was baby-sitting us had radioed ahead. We were expected, and as the strip appeared, we could see we had quite an audience waiting to see what would happen. I figured that we might as well give them a close look, and after firing a couple of red flares for an ambulance pick up, flew a couple of miles down the beach, slowly turned, eased down to a couple of hundred feet and buzzed the strip. I bought a dressing down from the base commander for that, but what the hell, it didn't seem right not to prove it would fly.

So far, so good; now all we had to do was land. It was a certainty I could not slow down to use flaps because I couldn't keep the nose up, so I flew about 5 miles down the beach again, eased around and still holding 200 ft and 180 mph, lined up on the runway, crossed my fingers and dropped the wheels, wondering what she would do. It worked out fine, except I had to pull full stick back in my lap just to counteract the wheel drag and add more throttle to keep the nose up so I would be able to fly her straight on to the ground. No go around—had to be right first time. By juggling the throttles the ground level approach looked OK, and just before we touched, I hit full throttle, which got the nose up enough for the main gear to hit first, snapped off power, shut idle cut-off to windmill the props to help slow down, and slid to a stop with no runway left. I taxied back to the mat strip, got out and looked—and damn near crapped. My gunner was right. No stabilizer and no rudder on the right side. If I had known it for real, I'd probably have crashed, because any fool knew a B-25 would just not fly in that condition.

Home sweet home for the 345th Bomb Group in New Guinea . . . Walter Besecker and Jack Bosley in the lap of luxury, ready for a welcome shower. Living conditions throughout the Pacific were made a bit better by the ever-present pyramidal tent that sprouted up at almost every AAF base. Navy pilots with their permanent quarters and legendary good food were the envy of army pilots, who could only dream of such things.

JOHN P. BRONSON

As war loomed closer in the Pacific, the stunning bare-metal aircraft of the Army Air Corps were overpainted with regulation olive drab and gray combat camouflage. Here 20th Pursuit Squadron Republic P-35As cruise on patrol over Clark Field in the summer of 1941 with the towering "cu" so typical of the area in the background. Army pilots flying these mid-1930s fighters on the eve of war knew the score. Max Louk, a 20th Squadron pilot, wrote home on 23 November, "I suppose you wonder what we think about the possibility of war. Well, we all hope it comes soon, because we are doomed at the start." Louk was killed on 8 December 1941 during the initial Japanese attack on the Philippines. Fighting the Japanese Zero on even terms would have to wait until more modern types could enter the theater. FRED ROBERTS VIA WILLIAM H. BARTSCH

By early 1941, the P-40 had become the standard Air Corps fighter, though some P-35s, and even some P-26s, continued to be maintained on the line. This P-40B of the 20th Pursuit Squadron is serviced at Clark Field, spring 1941. Basically the same type the Flying Tigers were flying, the Curtiss was the only fighter the United States had in the first six months of the war to hold off the Japanese. With foresighted candor, on 6 December Col. Hal George, knowing war was imminent, addressed the 3rd and 20th Pursuit Squadrons at the Clark Field Officer's Club: "You men are not necessarily a suicide squadron, but you are goddamn close to it!" When war came, army pilots, against tremendous

odds, patched together their shot-up airplanes, flew, then patched together what was left until there was nothing left and the Japanese occupied the Philippines. FRED ROBERTS VIA WILLIAM H. BARTSCH

Spring 1941 . . . the calm before the storm . . . a brand-new 11th Bomb Group B-17D Flying Fortress, assigned to Clark Field in the Philippines, is parked next to an A-27, an up-rated ground-attack version of the AT-6 trainer originally intended for Siam. There were few more idyllic duty stations in the prewar Army Air Corps than the Philippines, with a great climate, outstanding quarters, good flying, and some of the best golf courses in the Far East. War clouds began to darken the horizon that year, so much so that more than 75 percent of the B-17Ds built were flown out to the Hawaiian Islands and the Philippines to shake a fist at Japan's saber rattling in the Pacific. WILLIAM R. WRIGHT VIA WILLIAM H. BARTSCH

During the assault on Saipan, two escort carriers, the Manila Bay *and* Natoma Bay, *began launching AAF P-47Ds of the 318th Fighter Group on D-Day plus 7, 22 June 1944, to Aslito Airfield. Army pilots began flying close-support missions immediately, often through sniper fire from Japanese troops in the jungles southeast of the field as they took off. These 19th Squadron pilots head out for another mission on Saipan. Several missions per day were the norm, carrying bombs, rockets, and the normal load of .50-caliber machine-gun rounds. At night the field was shelled and shot at by hidden snipers, but the worst came on 25 June. The Japanese crept among the Thunderbolts to blow them up, then 300 more troops charged into the bivouac. Fighter pilots and ground crews became infantrymen in seconds and fought hand to hand until dawn. This wasn't the glamorous fighter pilot's war the press seemed to know all about.* PAUL THOMAS/BOB RICKARD*

Paul Thomas sits in his 19th Squadron, 318th Fighter Group P-47D on Saipan, awaiting start-up. An average mission for the group's Thunderbolt pilots during the fighting on the island was eighteen minutes from wheels in the wells to touchdown, which had a real kicker to it because only half-mission credit was awarded. Soon missions were being flown against artillery batteries hidden in caves and pillboxes on Tinian, only three miles across the channel from Saipan. During their first month of combat, pilots of the 19th and 73rd Squadrons flew more than 2,500 sorties, dropped 260 tons of bombs, and fired 500 rockets without sighting a single enemy aircraft. PAUL THOMAS/BOB RICKARD

A well-worn Army Air Forces Catalina on Okinawa. Less well known than the PBY in the navy, the OA-10A was the army version of this most famous of flying boats, assigned to Pacific units for air-sea rescue work. Quickly nicknamed "Dumbo" for their resemblance to Walt Disney's flying, floppy-eared cartoon elephant, the rescue Cats were the most loved of all aircraft in the theater. Before long, any rescue aircraft became a Dumbo regardless of type. It wasn't unusual for rescue crews to be up for days at a time looking for lost crews . . . there just wasn't anyone else to do the job, and Americans have always found it tormenting to give up looking for their own. JOHN A. WORTH

TOP *The Jolly Rogers, the 90th Bomb Group, flew their B-24 Liberators across the Pacific to some very distant targets for Fifth Air Force commander Lt. Gen. George C. Kenney, who praised the airplane as more useful to him than the B-17. The Lib · could fly a little faster, carry a few more bombs, and go a little farther than the Fort, a perfect combination for the vast stretches of ocean in the theater. There was no mistaking the group, commanded by flamboyant Col. Art Rogers, with the big Jolly Roger flying on their tails, clearly evident on this 400th Squadron B-24J at Mokmer Airdrome, Biak, in September 1944.* EDWARD F. EGAN

The 80th Fighter Squadron P-38J of Lt. William Fotheringham sits at Port Moresby, New Guinea. With the coming of the Lightning in late 1942, the air war in the Far East took a significant turn for the better. "Kenney's Kids" now had a fighter that could outrange and outfight anything the Japanese had, though virtually nothing could dogfight with a Zero or an Oscar. With both throttles forward, the '38 could walk away from the opposition, then turn around and slash back through with cannon and machine-gun fire. Pilots learned it had its weak points, but tactics were taught to its advantages and the weaknesses of Japanese aircraft. Its ability to come home on one engine saved many a pilot's life. BOB ROCKER VIA JACK FELLOWS

TOP *When the 345th Bomb Group, better known as the Air Apaches, went to war in New Guinea, it had a particularly talented and determined band of men, including Maj. Keith Dougherty, commander of the 500th Squadron, here in the cockpit of his B-25D. After some in-theater experimentation by innovators such as Col. Pappy Gunn, Mitchells were converted to multigun strafers. The Plexiglas noses were painted over and modified to carry .50-caliber machine guns in place of the bombardier. More guns were mounted to the sides in packs until the forward firepower was withering. Running across an enemy airfield on the deck in line-abreast formation, the Air Apaches could take out almost anything in one pass.* GEORGE J. FLEURY

BOTTOM *Bellying-in a shot-up airplane was not an unusual occurrence. This 501st Squadron, 345th Bomb Group B-25J was brought in wheels up at Clark Field in the Philippines on 12 July 1945 after having flown more than seventy-five missions since being assigned to the unit the previous October. The amazing thing about most B-25s brought in this way, unless heavily damaged by enemy fire, is that they could usually be lifted by a crane, their wheels lowered, towed away, repaired in short order, and put back on the line. The Mitchell was rugged and reliable, not to mention easy to fly and an excellent, stable strafing platform.* EDWARD F. EGAN

It didn't take long to age airplanes in combat, to the point they became a series of patchwork quilts and modifications. John Manders flew "The Gay Mare," a B-25D with the 501st Squadron, 345th Bomb Group, sitting here in its revetment at Nadzab, New Guinea, in May 1944. A modified strafer, the Mitchell has gone through more than its share of combat. The large metal panel in front of the side pack .50 calibers was meant to prevent buckling of the skin and stringers due to the continual blast of the guns. The Air Apaches were also antishipping experts . . . note the ship-kill marking . . . prowling the Pacific with excellent results.

T. K. LEWIS VIA VIVIAN LEWIS

TOP *The field modifications to transform the B-25 from a medium bomber to a low-level strafer are clearly evident here as the 501st Squadron of the Air Apaches heads for a target out of New Guinea in 1943. The Plexiglas nose on this B-25D has been painted over and the bombardier's position is loaded with forward-firing .50-caliber machine guns. There are side packs of two .50 calibers each on both sides of the fuselage, just visible beneath the No. 1 engine.* T. K. LEWIS VIA VIVIAN LEWIS

When P-51s and the long-range P-47Ns arrived in the Pacific in 1945, grueling, very long range (VLR) missions began, with Mustangs escorting B-29s all the way to Japan from Iwo Jima and Thunderbolts going on extreme-distance strike missions from Ie Shima. It was not unusual for pilots to sit in their cramped cockpits for more than ten hours, navigating over featureless ocean. Though the new Thunderbolts had folding rudder pedals so the pilot could stretch out, nothing made this punishment anything better than . . . punishment. This 464th Squadron, 507th Fighter Group P-47N sits in the sun on packed coral. Working on these airplanes could produce blisters to the touch on the hot aluminum skin . . . when painting the airframes, the paint often sizzled. JOHN A. WORTH

Mustangs of the 72nd Squadron, 21st Fighter Group, sit on the packed black volcanic ash of Iwo Jima, 1945. P-51s were near ideal aircraft for the very long range (VLR) mission of doing only one thing, escorting B-29s to Japan and back. In February and March 1945, the 15th and 21st Fighter Groups flew out to Iwo Jima in their P-51Ds as a part of VII Fighter Command. During the first VLR Empire Mission on 7 April 1945, escorting Superforts to Tokyo, Mustangs caught the intercepting Japanese by surprise and claimed twenty-one kills, five probables, and seven damaged for the loss of a single P-51 in the target area. It was a great beginning, but no one thought being cooped up for hours on end of sheer boredom, with a few brief moments of sheer terror, was great sport.
RUSS STAUFFER VIA CAMPBELL ARCHIVES

BOTTOM RIGHT *Ah, yes . . . mud . . . the ever-present commodity no one seemed to be able to sell or trade. This is the 345th Bomb Group's base at Dulag, Leyte, in the Philippines, 1945. The truck driver has a running start but the odds don't look good for getting through the "lil' ole mud puddle." The group's B-25s often suffered the same fate, though the runway and taxiways got first priority for keeping the mud at bay.*
GEORGE J. FLEURY

TOP *With the capture of Saipan and Tinian came the realization of the AAF's top priority in the Pacific: bombing the Japanese homeland with long-range B-29 Superfortresses. This pressurized, high-speed bomber was the wartime epitome of strategic bombardment doctrine, an airplane that could fly into the heart of enemy territory far from home base and deliver a significant bomb load. The horror and effectiveness embodied in this airplane came true with the fire raids of 1945, when entire cities would disappear overnight. These 313th Bomb Wing Superforts are spread out across Tinian in the spring of 1945. In the foreground, the dispersal area of the 9th Bomb Group, sits a brand-new B-29 with its load ready on the bulldozed revetment.* RUSS STAUFFER VIA CAMPBELL ARCHIVES

117 *Pacific Sweep*

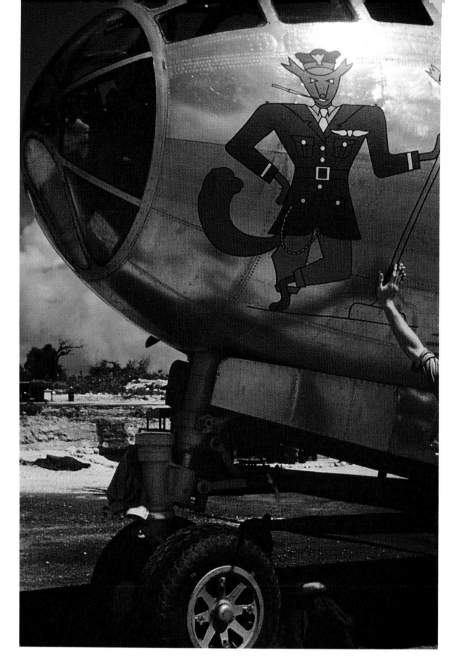

Superfortresses were ideal metal canvases for nose art, as this 29th Bomb Group B-29's zoot-suited army wolf, er pilot, shows at North Field, Guam. The B-29 was plagued with teething problems that followed it into combat. AAF chief Hap Arnold gave it his personal pressure to enter service, in spite of a tendency to develop engine fires due to improper cowling design. Yet it did the job with frightening efficiency from June 1944 to the end of the war in August 1945, laying waste to 175 square miles of urban area in 69 cities, leaving more than 9 million homeless. All Japan needed was a push over the brink, which happened over Hiroshima and Nagasaki with only two bombs. PAUL GRIBER VIA STAN PIET

TOP RIGHT *Dick Bong's P-38J, with twenty-seven kill flags on the nose, sits at Nadzab, New Guinea, in April 1944. By December, Richard Ira Bong had become America's ace of aces with forty confirmed kills. Though the Lightning carries the red markings of the 9th Squadron, 49th Fighter Group, Bong was actually attached to V Fighter Command by General Kenney, who allowed him to roam the Pacific at will in order to* stay in the thick of combat. Originally there was an enlargement of his fiancée's photo glued to the nose, but it blew off. Bong got home more than once on a single engine. During a mission over the Philippines, a P-38 pilot heard over the radio, "My engine's hit! I'm losing coolant! What'll I do?" The '38 pilot replied, "Calm down and feather it." Came the dejected reply, "Feather, hell . . . I'm flying a Mustang!" GEORGE J. FLEURY

Clark Field was a bustling place by 1945, a staging base for pressing the war toward Japan. It wasn't unusual to run into the other nations fighting the war, because they often stopped by for help or were assigned there on temporary duty. This Royal Navy Seafire, a tailhook-equipped version of the famous Spitfire, taxies across the field prior to returning to its ship. The tip of the hook is just visible under the belly, forward of the tail wheel. GEORGE J. FLEURY

One of the single most famous airplanes of all time, the "Enola Gay," which dropped the atomic bomb on Hiroshima, 6 August 1945, sits at North Field, Tinian. Flown by Paul Tibbets with a highly trained crew, the B-29 was attached to the 509th Composite Group, which had been preparing for the atomic mission since its inception. When "Bock's Car" dropped the next atom bomb on Nagasaki, 9 August, Japan fell to its knees and agreed to surrender. Without a doubt Japanese Admiral Isoroku Yamamoto's prediction reached the zenith of its fulfillment in the skies over these beautiful cities in August 1945. After receiving news of how the Pearl Harbor attack had gone, Yamamoto had said, "I fear all we have done is awaken a slumbering giant and fill him with a terrible resolve." The course of events over three and a half years proved him so very correct. R. W. TEED VIA FRED JOHNSEN

Co-pilot John Bronson's view running in on the target at Kavieng,
New Ireland, tracers streaming from
the nose of "Sandblasters." The Air
Apaches were incomparable low-level
artists, firing machine guns and cannon on the way in and dropping para-
frags or five-hundred-pound bombs
on the way out. There was no consid-
eration for doing anything but coming straight at a target at fifty feet in
the face of enemy fire. More than
seven hundred men had died by the
time the 345th went home. JOHN P.
BRONSON

THE GOOD WAR

End of an Era

DICK PERLEY
P-47 pilot, 50th Fighter Group

A large column of German troops in trucks with officers in cars showed up asking to surrender! Things were tense, but the German colonel was of the Signal Corps and not armed except for side arms, which I let him keep. I told him to go find somebody else to surrender to, like the army, because I was in the Air Corps. He turned the column around and off they went. Crazy times.

KEN KAILEY
C-47 pilot, 8th Troop Carrier Squadron

Shortly after VE Day, we made some freight runs up around Udine, Italy, northeast of Venice, and landed at a former German airfield. The American fields were usually just a strip with parallel taxi strips on both sides, joined to both ends of the runway, and the hardstands (single plane parking area) were spaced along the taxi strips. But the Germans . . . they went first class at this field—concrete runway! The concrete taxi strip went wandering off across the countryside, and their hardstands (surrounded by dirt banks) were spaced quite far apart along this strip. We sometimes had to taxi quite a distance to unload at one of the hardstands. It was a very pleasant experience—like driving a car along a concrete country road, wandering through the trees and green countryside. And very little traffic.

About the third or fourth time we came into this nice field, we noticed them breaking up the concrete and digging holes all along the runway. When we inquired as to what was going on, our troops informed us that they were merely digging up the mines that the Germans had failed to detonate when they pulled out! Although common sense tells you that it must have been all right because the Germans had been using the fields with those mines in place, it still gave me a very funny feeling to realize I had been landing on a mined runway.

DICK PERLEY
P-47 pilot, 50th Fighter Group

We seemed to have been, if not the first, close to it, troops coming into Camp Lucky Strike, which was one of several set up to send people home fast. Somehow enough trucks were found, all the personnel records gathered up in their four-foot stack, and we were off to our ship—the *Aiken Victory*. It was her maiden voyage, and it was still a sort of cargo ship, but fixed up with bunks. The sergeant major announced to me that he had arranged a special officer's "cabin." With a straight face he

When World War II ended, the nation took a collective sigh of relief after bearing what had appeared to be the unbearable for so long . . . then it let out a big whoop and celebrated, with reactions similar to those of these men of the 91st Photo Mapping Squadron upon seeing the headlines. OLE C. GRIFFITH

123

marched me to the psycho ward, which had about eight beds stacked to the ceiling. *Aiken Victory*—some name.

FRED WEINER
POW, Stalag Luft VI

It didn't take long to get back to the life in America. Yeah—you wanted to get started—you wanted to be a part of civilian life. While I was still in uniform, I met Edith (my wife). I wanted to get married, to get a job—so it didn't take long to get going. There are some things that are hard to tell somebody about the fun we had in the prison camps. In order to go steady with me, Edith promised to let her friends meet the guy before she got serious with him. We had a double date at the Paramount to see Frank Sinatra.

We're in a line and have to wait two hours to get in. We're talking and it turns out the other guy was a POW at Stalag 17B. Here I was a POW from Stalag Luft VI—we started in with the stories—laughing and telling anecdotes about prison camp life. People gathered all around us to hear us talk. We could hear them in the background saying, "Didn't they say they were in a prison camp?!"

CORRINE WALL
wife of B-24 co-pilot

Before we left, the boys took us up to the field and showed us their plane. It looked so big to us at that time. We went up to the doorway and it didn't seem very comfortable inside. Since the pilot was from Texas, he called the plane *San Antone Rose,* "like the song." I remember they named each one of the engines with our names. They said, "That one's Lucille, that one's Corrine, and Marie and Louise!" Well, they left and that was it. We had time for a few letters, and just before he went on his last mission, Jack told me he was having a bad case of sinus problems. He was going to be sent home!

On June 12, 1944, we got word that the ship had gone down and the crew was missing in action. Mr. Wall told me, "Corrine, I will take care of all these matters," when the news came about Jack. The army wrote to my father-in-law in Bridgeport, Illinois, so he would get all the news first, then send it on to me in California. That's the way he wanted it. I don't know how many planes went down that day, but it was supposed to be one of the real bad ones. I thought all the boys went down together and were prisoners in the same place over there—in truth, we never really knew too much about what happened to the crew.

STAN HUTCHINS
B-24 pilot, 484th Bomb Group

Actually, I found our actions in World War II the humane thing we could do under the circumstances. Our true motives were later, in victory, spelled out in the Marshall Plan, support of the United Nations and the General Agreement on Tariffs and Trade, which got rid of barriers to free trade with our former enemies. I did regret our low CEP [circular error probability, or ability to get a concentration of bombs on target] but more because of lack of damage to the aim points than to collateral damage in the area. I don't know what to say about those who have "second thoughts" or revisionist endings based on "more humane" tactics. With the bombers we had, this was about the only way to do the job.

RUTH HATTON
wife of B-24 waist gunner

Many of the GI's with us were returning from overseas. You might expect war weariness in their demeanor; their eyes told a different story. I stood and looked over the crowded train and saw an intensity in their faces; not of anxiety, but more of a determined look. The weariness of body did not seem to extend to the expression in their eyes. It seemed to say, "There is another job to be done and I'm going to do it." There was no exhilaration . . . no back pounding . . . just a thoughtful but serious intensity. I feel that intensity and determination gave the drive that changed the course of events in the following era. We had an era of hope—of rebuilding—of positive expansion. I saw the same look in Hy's eyes many times.

Daytona Beach . . . yes, sir! Once settled back in the United States with his wife, Dorothy Helen, Jeep Crowder wasted little time in making up for lost time. Combat in P-40s and A-36s over North Africa, Sicily, and Italy had been more than rough, particularly as the Crowders had been married a very short time before Jeep shipped out. Dorothy Helen is on the right, money out, ready to choose from a variety of pure American delights . . . whatever the stomach can stand.

J. P. CROWDER VIA DOROTHY HELEN CROWDER

The occupation of Japan was a great surprise to Americans, who still found it hard to understand their former enemy. With rare exception, when the emperor ordered the nation to surrender, its people viewed it in the same light as being ordered to war—they would do it with a near fanatical devotion. As a result, Americans were welcomed with candy and flowers, regardless of the horrendous destruction they had visited on the homeland. The hard-working Japanese set about rebuilding their land, fueled with American dollars, with the same energy of the soldier who fought to the death. The Diet Building in Tokyo remained the center of government, this time presided over by Gen. Douglas MacArthur and surrounded by army vehicles and Military Police.
MARK BROWN/USAFA

Sights such as this German PzKw.V Panther tank next to the very sad bombed-out cathedral at Cologne were common. Germany had been blown to rubble, visible at its worst in the large cities. With great foresight, Harry Truman backed the Marshall Plan to rebuild this former enemy and, hopefully, to avoid repeating history. The post—World War I Versailles Treaty had created the seeds of a bitter and angry harvest but a scant two decades later . . . "sow the wind, reap the whirlwind." MARK BROWN/USAFA

TOP *Paris bounced back out of war to regain its place as the Continent's garden spot . . . it still overwhelmed boys from down on the farm. Cars were scarce, so bicycles were standard transportation, evident from these tricycle taxi cabs parked near the Arc de Triomphe in late 1945. From sidewalk cafés and bistros to the Follies Bergere, Americans lost themselves in a city that seemed to have something for everyone and almost no hint of the war.* MARK BROWN/USAFA

Even in the midst of so much destruction, there were marvelous remnants of the Old World. American military trucks became a fixture, evident here in the streets of Linz, Austria. Though there was little doubt the conquerors could be the focus of resentment on the part of the residents, and vice versa, both sides became accustomed to the situation, usually making the best of it. Close to starvation, Germans sought any job possible from the Americans, even if the pay was food alone. It was a difficult and sad time.
MARK BROWN/USAFA

Postwar flying time was doled out to pilots in minimal increments . . . after all, there was no need to do much flying without an enemy. When they did get to go flying, fighter pilots took to the classic pasttimes of buzzing towns, flying under bridges, and sightseeing. A year and a half after the surrender, the occupation air force in Germany was getting slim, so the few airplanes left were boredom fighters indeed. George McWilliams demonstrates the art on this spectacular hop over the Bavarian Alps in his 397th Squadron, 368th Fighter Group P-47D in the fall of 1946. His wingman, Arthur Houston, who shot this photo, had flown but a single combat mission before the war ended, then spent almost two years trying to feel useful. ARTHUR O. HOUSTON

With surrender came occupation of the defeated nations. Warplanes were quickly turned into transportation, or scrapped outright. This B-25 parked next to the fire brigade at Gablingen, *Germany, was requisitioned by the 355th Fighter Group, then stripped of all its armor and guns to make it a "fat cat," an airplane used for supply runs or touring Germany. There was* *very little to do in 1945 without a war going on, resulting in severe limits on flying time. Pilots found ships like this a perfect outlet until getting sent back home.* ALEXANDER C. SLOAN

Jammed in, sitting on duffel bags and baggage, combat-worn pilots from the 27th Fighter Bomber Group begin the first leg home in an over-loaded C-47. Though the hours and hours across the Atlantic were exhausting, with no comfort to speak of, no food, and constant high-noise levels, it sure beat the long trip in an oceangoing vessel . . . anything was worth it just to get home a little faster. J. P. CROWDER VIA DOROTHY HELEN CROWDER

The main airport at Paris, Le Bourget, remained bombed out for some time, though its runways and parking areas were quickly useable after the liberation of the city in August 1944. A Free French Air Force Westland Lysander, with the Cross of Lorraine over the national roundel, sits on the ramp. The Allies supplied the Free French, under Charles de Gaulle, with squadrons of aircraft to fight the Germans and their Vichy French collaborators. These airplanes remained with the French to form the basis for postwar expansion, something they took quite seriously. MARK BROWN/USAFA

ABOVE *With little shelter, and less food, the Japanese struggled to manage a bare existence. This former Japanese Army soldier wears his old uniform, most likely the best set of clothes he owns, on a road southwest of Nagoya as he brings to market what he has managed to grow. In spite of wartime atrocities and the fanatical spirit of the Kamikaze, Americans grew to respect the people they now ruled, forming friendships and partnerships that endured.* MARK BROWN/ USAFA

Returning vets came home to new, sparkling airports of the future—like Washington National with the Great Silver Fleet of Eastern Airlines on the ramp just after the war. Aviation was going to be available to everyone, even a small plane in every garage. Though private aviation failed to boom, the airlines went from strength to strength, shrinking the world for the average citizen as it had for those in the services. EDWARD B. RICHIE

September 1945 . . . personnel of the 406th Fighter Group await the order to board a C-47 at Nordholz, Germany, for rotation back to the Z.I.—Zone of Interior—the good ole USA. Clearly the worn old Gooney has seen some hard use, sporting varying shades of fading paint and patches on its fabric control surfaces. Who cared? It managed to fly in on its own, didn't it? It would get back out on its own. No one wanted to pass up a seat. JOHN QUINCY VIA STANLEY J. WYGLENDOWSKI

RIGHT *What a swell welcome . . . as the victory ship* Westminster Victory *approaches New York harbor full of ETO veterans in 1946, an army tugboat comes alongside to put the icing on the cake. Home-front Americans couldn't do enough to make their servicemen feel proud of what they had accomplished, and red carpets were thrown across just about every threshold available. Everyone was sure, for a brief shining moment, war among mankind was over.* JOHN QUINCY VIA STANLEY J. WYGLENDOWSKI

The Good War

TOP LEFT AND RIGHT *Coming home conjured up a flood of memories, from the girl back home to . . .* food! *From the time they left, most members of the armed services, and every POW, dreamed of coming back to that panorama of American food they had left behind. When Sgt. Cal Sloan of the 1066th Signal Company hit Los Angeles on his way home in 1945, he lovingly took out his camera and captured a cornerstone of the American way of life, from Simon's Drive-In to the Brown Derby, the watering hole of Hollywood's most famous. The visual impact was almost as good as eating . . . well, not really.* ALEXANDER C. SLOAN

The end of the line . . . Kingman, Arizona, late 1946. This was one of the largest of the thirty aircraft grave-yards set up to handle the excess of war. Trying to get rid of tens of thousands of airplanes was almost more than the War Assets Administration could handle, yet anyone could buy one. All you had to do was walk in, inspect the aircraft of your choice with log books provided, answer a few minor questions, sign your name a couple of times, pay for it "as is, where is," and fly away with full tanks. There were no questions about the buyer's ability to fly such fire-breathers. If you were a veteran, you could even get a loan with 15 percent down, balance payable in 36 monthly installments at 4 percent interest. There was no rush of buyers for P-38s and Corsairs at $1,250, B-17s at $13,750, or Hellcats for $3,500. Hollywood pilot Paul Mantz put in a bid of $55,000 for 475 aircraft at Walnut Ridge, Arkansas . . . there were no other takers. He flew as many of them away as he could, then scrapped out the rest. He figured the airplanes had originally cost the tax-payer $117 million. By the late 1940s all the rest had been smelted back into pots and pans. BYRON TRENT

When pilots and crews got home, they saw that wartime leaps in aviation technology had borne more fruit than the ability to deliver mass destruction. This brand-new Lockheed C-69 Constellation, though birthed by the Army Air Forces, was actually the modern airliner ready to jump from the stalls and move the world into the modern age. Its sleek lines and powerful engines were the shape of things to come. The major airlines, released from wartime conscription, wasted no time in using it on the free market.

OLE C. GRIFFITH

A vision of things to come—a brand-new Lockheed P-80A Shooting Star firing up on the line at Wright Field, Ohio, the AAF's flight test center. With the jet engine, the great, golden age of the propeller came to an end and aviation's second era began. It was disorienting to many coming home . . . they had assumed they were flying the hottest stuff in the world, only to find out their beloved mounts were antiques. World War II proved to be the ideal matrix for the acceleration of a technological revolution that spread to all disciplines, changing institutions across the planet . . . nothing has been the same since. OLE C. GRIFFITH

When there was nothing left to be done with airplanes but burn them up, so be it. Local Germans, including some former Luftwaffe fighter pilots, were hired to melt down this pile of 354th Fighter Group Mustangs and bury the leftovers at Herzoge-naurach. What the Germans had been unable to do for several years—destroy the U.S. Army Air Forces in Europe—Americans now paid them to do. Indeed, war made no sense and sometimes peace even less. HERBERT R. RUTLAND, JR.

BOTTOM LEFT Almost-new Thunderbolts of the 58th Fighter Group sit among the lines and lines of AAF war machines on the ramp at Clark Field, with Mt. Pinatubo in the background. With no war to fight, the tools became excess baggage . . . actually, a real headache. Many remained lined up for years until finally scrapped. Others were bulldozed into holes and buried, or into piles and burned until slag. America had pushed its industrial capacity so hard it was difficult to turn the hose off—planes kept rolling off the assembly lines even after the war ended. VIA DONALD A. SODERLUND, JR.

The navy couldn't bring all of its airplanes home either, so orders came down to get rid of certain types, like this obsolete FM-2 Wildcat being pushed off "suicide cliff" at Marpi Point, Saipan, in 1945. Someone thought to look in the log books . . . it had amassed but twenty-five hours of flying time since new. Many other types were pushed overboard at sea before the carriers came home to roost. A great deal of American warmaking potential had become just so much junk, useless in a world that would never see war again. EDWARD W. SIMPSON, JR.

ABOUT THE AUTHOR

Jeffrey L. Ethell has logged more than four thousand hours of flight time in a wide variety of aircraft around the world, from the Corsairs and Flying Fortresses of the World War II era to the most advanced of the military's current aircraft inventory. He has also participated in combat operations with various nations to gather firsthand information on air tactics and weapons effectiveness. He has published more than a thousand magazine articles on aviation history and more than forty books, including *One Day in a Long War, F-15 Eagle, Air War South Atlantic,* and *Smithsonian Frontiers of Flight,* which is the companion volume to the Discovery Channel series of the same name. He has served as the correspondent for ABC's *Wide World of Flying* series, the writer/on-screen host for the *Roaring Glory* and *Flying the Jets* series, and the technical adviser and script writer for A&E's *First Flights.* In addition, he lectures across the United States and overseas at war colleges, military establishments, and aircraft corporations, analyzing the wartime arena, both past and present. Known for his hard-hitting, truthful analyses, he continues to fly extensively with the military services.